Out in God's Country

Out in God's Country

Historical Sketches of
Colfax County, New Mexico

Larry Murphy

Cover image, book design, typesetting, and editing: Steve Lewis
    Eagle Trail Press, Apache Junction, Arizona.

Library of Congress Control Number: 2021949820
ISBN: 978-0-9974267-6-2

Contents

Beginnings

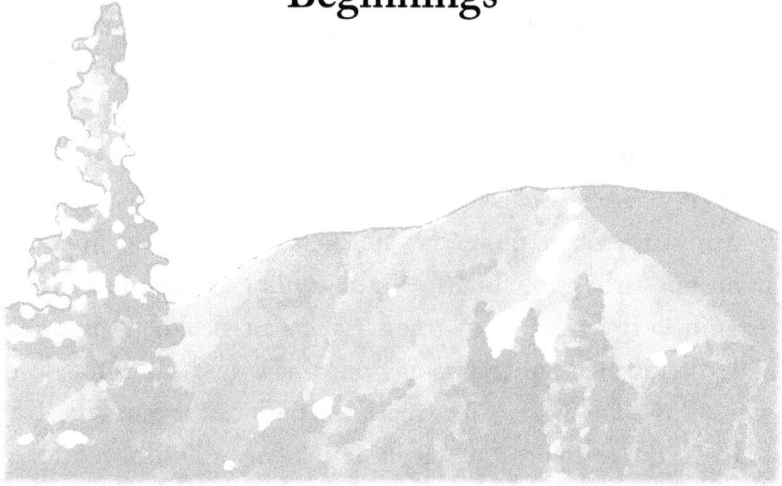

A Land of Pioneers

The history of Colfax County and northern New Mexico, like that of the whole West, is full of pioneers. Centuries before any European undertook the conquest of North America, primitive Indians camped beside our cool Rocky Mountain streams and hunted game on our broad plains. Carrying the cross of Rome and the flag of Spain, valiant conquerors soon trekked northward from Mexico. Equally venturesome were the Americans who pushed westward from the Atlantic colonies. Wagons overflowing with trade goods were shortly crossing the Vermejo, Cimarron, and Rayado Rivers on their way to Santa Fe. From the mountains, fur trappers' campfires sparkled in the night.

Eventually settled under the leadership of Charles Beaubien and Lucien Maxwell, the "Kingdom of Colfax" attracted a new brand of pathfinder. Miners and cattlemen, storekeepers and lumbermen resisted Indian attack, shivered through cold moun-

1

tain winters and sweltered beneath the summer sun to establish communities along the Sangre de Cristo Mountains. Elizabethtown, Cimarron, Springer, Maxwell, Raton, and a dozen other towns bear witness to their success. Aided by railroad and highway construction, the region has more recently become a center of ranching, coal mining, and recreational activities. From schools, churches, and civic leaders come programs for an even brighter future.

Everywhere evidence of the past appears. Arrowheads or pottery unearthed by a plow may aid the scientist in learning more about our earliest inhabitants. In crumbling adobe ruins or once magnificent Victorian mansions, a cavalry soldier, mountain man, or rancher-capitalists may once have laid plans for developing this land. Wagon ruts mark the path of the Santa Fe Trail, while in the museums at Raton, Cimarron, Rayado, Elizabethtown, and Springer, the tools of a past generation are on display.

Mural depicting pioneers migrating westward, by Edwin Blashfield.
Library of Congress Prints and Photographs Division, Public Domain Images.

Deep shafts and huge rock piles remind visitors of hard-working miners. Place names like Maxwell, Dawson, French, and Springer commemorate men of particular ability and prominence. Only the area's current greatness memorializes the thousands of other settlers.

From scattered and varied sources comes information about Colfax County's past. Geological and archaeological investigations have taught us much about the natural setting and native inhabitants. Torn, faded Spanish or Mexican records report the advance of conquerors or the bravery of settlers. Rooms full of dusty newspapers in Raton's County Courthouse or the New Mexico State Museum chronicle the daily events of early New Mexico. Records from the United States government's Cimarron Indian Agency detail nearly two decades of progress, while the corporate records of the Maxwell Land Grant Company expand this history to nearly a century.

Other historians have also aided in plowing the earth for planting, including Jim Pearson, William Keleher, and Father Stanley who all contributed greatly. Finally, there are those still among us whose stories of the people and events of the past prove invaluable. Narciso Abreu, Victor Van Lint, Thomas W. Schomburg, Ada Springer Davis, Katherine D. McCormick, Mary Lail, and Fred Lambert are but a few of the many to whom this author owes thanks.

With the aid of such documents, books, and memories, the story can be unfolded. A thousand years of uncounted denizens have passed through our country, and all were pioneers.

Mountains, Mesas, and Plains

Situated along the magnificent Sangre de Cristo Mountains, Colfax County offers scenery seldom equalled and rarely surpassed in the Southwest. In the east, broad plains which stretch as far as the eye can see are broken by mesas protruding skyward.

Along the county's western side are the Rocky Mountains. Rapidly rising to altitudes exceeding 12,000 feet, they have lured miners, lumbermen, and ranchers, and more recently the tourists. Men have described the area's panoramic beauty ever since they first occupied it.

Over a century ago, in 1841, a Santa Fe trader crossing from Missouri was cheered by the first distant appearance of the mountains.

> From day to day, the beauty of the scenery increased, and when within twenty miles, the reflection of the sun through the melting snow that eternally crowns their highest peaks is splendid beyond description. Here the traveler beholds a chain of many hundred, nay thousands, of miles piled up as it were until they reach to heaven.

Eons of geologic development crafted northern New Mexico's underlying rock structure. Cooling and cracking processes deep within the earth sent molten rock spewing through the hardening crust, bending and arching existing formations. Streams which formed in the highlands eroded the rock, however, and deposited sand and gravel along river beds until each range had been worn down. After subsequent uplifting the process repeated itself until a variety of geographic formations had been intermingled in the mountains.

Several distinctive geographical features resulted from these processes. Extending southward from Colorado to Ute Park, the Park Plateau is a huge sandstone belt cut by narrow, shallow valleys. Best observed from US Highway 64 between Raton and Cimarron, these formations contain some of the richest coal beds in the Southwest.

A chain of high mountains made up primarily of dacite porphyry stretches from Little Costilla Peak southward to La Grulla Mesa. Chiseled by rushing streams and interspersed by lush mountain meadows, its particular riches include lumber

Topography of Colfax County where the mountains meet the plains.
US Geological Survey, Professional Paper 505, Plate 1, 1964.

and precious minerals such as gold. A thick lava flow created the flat-topped mesas of southern Colfax County, where upland meadows offer unparalleled summer grazing for livestock. Finally, the Las Vegas Plateau drops slowly away from the mountains to form the area's southeastern flatlands where irrigated farming and ranching thrive.

Just as varied as its geography are the county's flora and fauna. On the flatlands, antelope and jack rabbits abound where vast herds of buffalo once roamed.

Replacing prairie grasses, Piñon pines and junipers grow in the foothills, while belts of Ponderosa pine, white fir, and spruce dominate at higher altitudes. Deer, elk, and bear are joined there by a variety of ground squirrels, rabbits, birds, and other wildlife. High atop the loftiest peaks only the hardiest plants and animals can withstand strong winds, low humidity, and bitter cold.

The Earliest Inhabitants

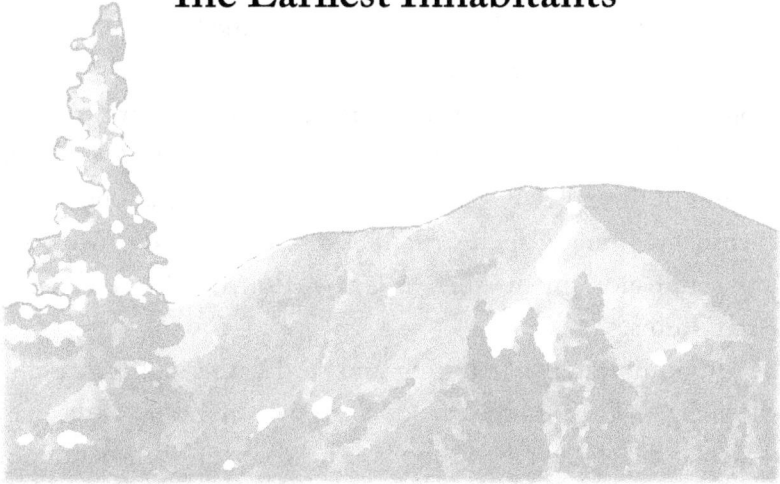

The Pueblo People

Colfax County's first pioneers were Indians, part of a large but diverse primitive society which occupied most of the American continent long before Europeans arrived.

All evidence indicates that these people first crossed the narrow Bering Straits from Siberia to the Alaskan mainland thousands of years before Christ. Slowly migrating southward over the years, they eventually reached even to the southern extremes of South America.

Many different aboriginal groups have inhabited Colfax County over centuries. Those from the Plains loved to hunt and fight, while other more peaceful people took up agricultural pursuits and lived in semi-permanent adobe dwellings. Arriving from 1000 to 1700 AD, the native groups significantly impeded European settlement of the area until the last decades of the nineteenth century.

One of the earliest of these groups to cross the Sangre de Cristo Mountains were the forefathers of the Pueblo Indians who now inhabit adobe villages along the Rio Grande River throughout New Mexico. Known to archaeologists as the Anasazi or "Ancient Ones," these Indians slowly developed the high cultural level for which they are now known. At their earliest homes in Colorado, the ancestors of the Pueblos lived in primitive caves where their finest crafts were crude baskets. Slowly over long periods of time they began to erect larger stone or adobe homes, eventually building such structures as can be visited at national parks and monuments such as Chaco Canyon, Mesa Verde, or Aztec Ruins.

The importance of hunting and seed gathering decreased as the villagers irrigated their fields to grow corn, beans, and squash which became their basic foods. The colorful, well-made pottery which replaced baskets has been justifiably acclaimed for its artistic qualities. Woven from cultivated cotton, Indian cloth

Taos Pueblo as it appeared in the late 1880s with natives posing near beehive-shaped ovens (*ornos*) and on rooftops accessible from ladders. Sangre de Cristo Mountains in the background.

Library of Congress Prints and Photographs Division, Public Domain Images.

garments amazed even the Spanish conquerors, while native yucca fibers were woven into serviceable sandals. Elaborate religious rituals held in characteristic underground *kivas* developed around such an agricultural economy.

It is not known when the first Pueblo warrior ventured across the mountains east of the Rio Grande River, but archaeological evidence indicates their arrival as early as 1000 AD. Perhaps searching for more plentiful game supplies on the plains, hunting parties probably explored most of Colfax County, mixing with other Indians in the area, camping for short periods along our streambeds, perhaps spending entire summers here.

Pueblo painted pottery unearthed in the Cimarron area has aided scientists in dating native occupation of the region. Farming pursuits, sandal manufacturing, and other Pueblo traits seem to have been passed on to the more permanent residents of Colfax County. But the Pueblo penetration was never permanent. Returning to their better-watered valley homes, they left the fertile canyons and game-rich hills facing the Great Plains to other highly nomadic residents.

Folsom Man

While Anasazi people were moving southward along the Rio Grande and eastward across the Sangre de Cristo Mountains, other Indians were entering Colfax County from the Great Plains. One of the earliest and most famous discoveries of early man in all of North America was made in 1926 near Folsom in western Union County, New Mexico. Scientists' previous theory that man had occupied the New World for only a few thousand years was suddenly shattered by this discovery.

Along a seasonal branch of the Dry Cimarron River excavations revealed prehistoric bison bones in association with man-made spears and arrow points. Using their knowledge of when these prehistoric bison became extinct, archaeologists estimated

Prehistoric bison bones *in situ* with Folsom point.
National Scouting Museum Collection, Cimarron, New Mexico.

that "Folsom Man" lived between 10,000 and 25,000 years ago. Other Folsom points found throughout the Plains indicate that this civilization extended over much of mid-America.

Although no Folsom points are known to have been found in Colfax County, the men who made them may well have trekked across the area in search of game. Workmen moving material for a road at the Philmont Ranch near Cimarron found the fossilized remains of prehistoric mammoths near Urraca Creek. These finds demonstrate that many types of prehistoric animals might have been successfully hunted by early man in the area.

After the demise of Folsom Man, a prolonged drought prevented occupation of the Plains for several thousand years. But the new Indian groups who arrived by 2500 BC also had a hunting-oriented economy. Animals were in such short supply, however, that seed and root gathering was also necessary to survive. The women may even have cultivated small garden plots along creek beds.

Prior to the coming of the horse as a means of transportation, these Indians had a culture far less colorful than that of subsequent Plains inhabitants. Crude brush, wood, or stone houses provided little comfort, but over time dwellings increased in size and permanence. From Indians moving onto the flatlands from the west they also learned to make pottery, usually unpainted and always poorer in quality than that of the Pueblos.

With the Pueblo people living to the west and the Plains Indians in the east, the area within Colfax County fostered a unique marginal culture that mixed traits from both. Residing in many of the region's fertile foothill valleys, these people were the first to remain over extended periods of time. From archaeological investigations carried out by scientists from the Museum of New Mexico and elsewhere, we have learned much about these Ponil People.

The Ponil People

For three hundred years or more, marginal Plains-Pueblo groups occupied Colfax County at least seasonally and perhaps permanently. Avoiding both the hot, dry plains and the colder mountains, they resided in the fertile and well-watered valleys which intrude into the Park Plateau. Because the most extensive studies have been conducted in the Ponil River watershed, however, they are called the "Ponil people."

Where these Indians came from is a mystery. While some archaeologists think they were Plains tribes who learned from their Pueblo neighbors to make pottery and build dwellings, others believe that people living along the Rio Grande River may have been unsuccessful at maintaining an agricultural economy and were forced to move east to depend on hunting. The area may have been an Indian frontier where more primitive conditions prevailed. A third alternative is that an unknown independent civilization moved into the area and assumed whatever characteristics best suited the living conditions.

Colfax County's first homes varied widely in construction, size, and permanence. The earliest arrivals camped beneath natural sandstone overhangs, frequently adding interior walls or stone pavements to make them more comfortable. The later slab house represents a much more complex building technique. Flat sandstone rocks were stacked around the edge of the multi-room dwelling, reaching a height of almost two feet. Supported by a number of posts irregularly spaced inside, a heavy timbered earth and brush-covered roof kept out the rain and wind. Pueblo influences were seen in the circular underground pit houses, similar to those found along the Rio Grande valley.

The Ponil people made their living from hunting as well as farming. Corn grown along their streams could be roasted or

Petroglyphs in Ponil Canyon near Cimarron, New Mexico,
perhaps representing a great river valley with many side canyons.

National Scouting Museum Collection, Cimarron, New Mexico.

ground into meal. Beans and squash were other important crops. They also used tiny arrowheads to kill the small game which were as common in the area then as they are now.

The local handicrafts found by archaeologists are notably inferior to those of the Pueblos. Although these Indians imported pottery from the Pueblos, their own wares typically consisted of brittle, unpainted pottery that was crude by comparison. Occasionally baskets, yucca sandals, and even leather items have been discovered during excavations. These are invaluable for learning more about the lives of early natives.

Most famous among the Indians' artistic legacy are the petroglyphs or "Indian Writings." Found along many of the protected sandstone cliffs in the foothill country, they have not as yet been deciphered. Perhaps designed as religious symbols, picture histories, route maps, or even casual doodles, they may never be fully understood.

Where the Ponil people went is just as mysterious as where they came from. Perhaps driven away by invaders or forced to move because of drought, they had disappeared by 1400 AD, leaving Colfax County open for subsequent Indian arrivals and the eventual conquest by European explorers.

Conquerors and Marauders

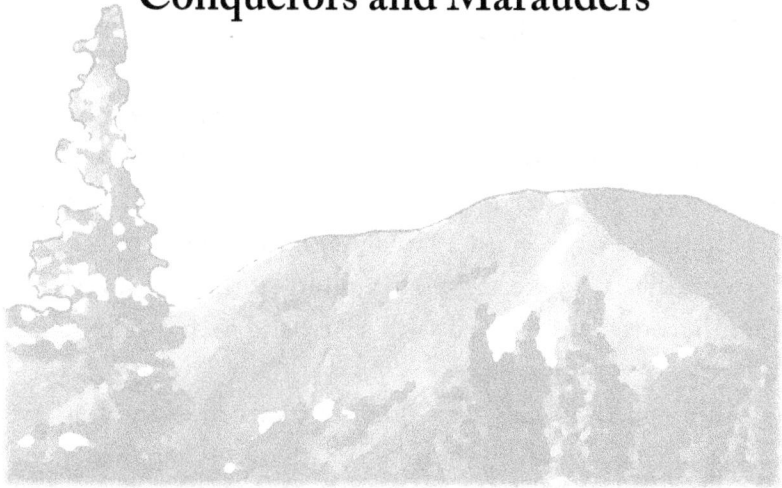

Northward with Cross and Sword

In less than a century Spanish conquerors spread European language and culture through vast regions of the New World. Brave, fearless, and even foolhardy men subdued Indian tribes from Peru to New Mexico, establishing towns, planting mission churches, and promoting their cultural values. Catholicism became the prevailing religion and Spanish the most prominent language.

The first conquistador to visit New Mexico was Alvar Nuñez Cabeza de Vaca. Departing the West Indies for Florida, his expedition ran into considerable difficulties. Many boats were wrecked along the coast, and a Gulf hurricane destroyed log rafts on which they planned to return to safety. Tossed aground in what would become south Texas, Cabeza de Vaca and three companions—including a slave called Little Stephen—began a long and wearisome trek back to civilization. When they crossed southern

New Mexico they heard exaggerated stories of the Pueblos. Visions of a high civilization, perhaps "another Mexico," gleamed in Cabeza de Vaca's mind as he entered the Mexican capital.

When he heard these tales of reported riches, Viceroy Antonio de Mendoza, the political head of Mexico, sent an exploratory expedition under Fray Marcos de Niza. Accompanied by Little Stephen, the party travelled rapidly northward. Stephen scouted ahead and he was to send back crosses to the priests varying in size according to the importance of his discoveries. Fray Marcos reported that he received a cross the size of a man and, rushing forward, he saw a great city with multi-storied houses. He said that the streets were paved with silver, and each dwelling had a doorway of turquoise.

Although historians have questioned whether the friar even saw a pueblo, his stories resulted in the most famous Spanish expedition. Led by Francisco Vasquez de Coronado, the large government-sponsored party left Mexico in 1540. But only disappointment awaited them, as Coronado found only mud pueblos instead of fantastically rich cities. The expedition remained in New Mexico for nearly two years, during which time the Spaniards ventured westward as far as the Grand Canyon and the Arizona-California border. In the east, a party crossed New Mexico and the Texas panhandle to Kansas before returning to the Mexican capital.

Not until the first years of the seventeenth century were permanent Spanish settlements established in New Mexico. A large colonizing party under Juan de Oñate brought women and children as well as sheep, cattle, and horses into the area. By 1610 they had founded Santa Fe, later renowned as the oldest capital city in America. Spanish civilization slowly spread along the Rio Grande Valley.

The Pueblo Revolt of 1680 temporarily expelled the Europeans, but within a decade the Spanish had reconquered the area.

Spanish soldiers and priests on the march, by Frederic Remington.
Library of Congress Prints and Photographs Division, Public Domain Images.

Once New Mexico was safe from internal uprisings, it was possible to expand into the northeastern section of the territory. Not for long would Colfax County belong to the Indian tribes which inhabited the area where the mountains meet the plains.

The Jicarilla Apaches

While Spaniards were moving northward toward Colfax County, Indian tribes filled the void left by the Ponil people's departure. One group which had arrived in the area by 1700 were the Jicarilla Apache—pronounced "hick-ah-REE-ya."

These Indians were part of a huge linguistic family called Athabascans. From their original homeland somewhere in central Canada, they pushed south along several routes. One large band reached southern California, while another became the fierce Navajos of the Four Corners area. Among the Apache proper, the Jicarillas remained furthest north. The Lipan group moved into Texas, and the Western and Chiricahua Apaches (most famous for their unrelenting opposition to encroaching

17

settlers) lived in southern New Mexico and Arizona.

Much like earlier Ponil residents, the Jicarilla culture combined traits of both hunters and growers. Costumes and other aspects of their material culture resembled that of the Plains Indians. Buffalo hunting was an important economic pursuit. They also stalked deer and drove antelope herds into box canyons where they could be easily killed. Yet agriculture also developed. Fields were cleared, dams built, and ditches dug so that extensive irrigated farming was possible. While corn was their principal product, pumpkins, peas, beans, and even tobacco were also cultivated.

No elaborate political system unified the Jicarillas into anything approaching a formal tribe. Family groups moved from one camping spot to another in an independent search for better fields or more plentiful supplies of game. Anyone claiming to be the "chief" held his position only because of personal abilities or an attractive personality. The single warrior was most important in a society which emphasized individualism.

Jicarilla Apache encampment in the 1870s. Edward Curtis Collection.
Library of Congress Prints and Photographs Division, Public Domain Images.

A happy, positive people, the Jicarillas prospered in their Colfax County homes. Plenty of game was available in the mountains where the Indians spent many a summer camped in the grassy meadows along the eastern Sangre de Cristos. During the fall and winter their brush huts appeared along the lower Sweetwater, Rayado, Cimarron, Ponil, and Vermejo Rivers. By April or May, tall corn stalks had grown up in their fields. Occasional hunting parties which ventured onto the plains carried back huge quantities of buffalo meat.

The Moache Utes

A second Indian group which occupied Colfax County by the time the Spaniards arrived were the Moache Utes—pronounced "mo-AH-tsi." Arriving from the northwest, they were originally enemies of the Jicarillas, but in later years the two tribes mingled together peacefully, intermarrying and exchanging cultural characteristics until it became difficult to differentiate between them.

Unlike the Apache, the Utes were originally mountain dwellers. Linguistically related to the Shoshonean tribes in the intermountain states of Nevada, Utah, and Colorado, they had long resided in the rugged mountains, broad plateaus, and high deserts of western America. But sometime before 1700 they too were forced southward. In search of game and a less rigorous existence, they spilled into the mountains of Colorado and northern New Mexico. Among the southern Utes were the Weeminuche and Capote bands who resided in the western San Juan country, and the Moaches of Colfax and Taos Counties in New Mexico.

The Moache Utes were never very numerous or very prosperous. Only a few hundred ever occupied Colfax County and these lived a hand-to-mouth existence. Starvation threatened whenever game supplies diminished because of bad weather or the presence of other marauding tribes. They apparently never learned to farm or even to maintain seasonally permanent homes, so the

Mounted party of Ute hunters breaking camp.
Library of Congress Prints and Photographs Division, Public Domain Images.

extinction of the buffalo and the reduction of other game meant ultimate defeat.

Every phase of Ute life revolved around hunting, and boys were encouraged to play with bows, arrows, and spears almost as soon as they were born. As they neared adulthood, Ute teenagers accompanied older relatives on the hunts. Whatever game they found was slaughtered and the blood rubbed onto the youngster's body, thereby transferring the characteristics of the animal to the young hunter. If it was a deer, he became a tireless stalker. Coyote blood made him clever and crafty, while a mountain lion's blood made him powerful and sly. Girls learned campcraft skills. Cleaning game, tanning hides, cooking or drying meat were necessary abilities in a Ute household.

Religion also reflected economic concerns. The Ute's supreme deity was associated with the life-giving sun or the wolf, nature's ablest hunter. The moon and stars, eagles, elk, buffalo, lightning, and coyotes all represented supernatural forces.

Much evidence of Ute occupation exists in Colfax County. Ute Park, a beautiful grassy meadow at the entrance to the Cimarron Canyon narrows, was a favorite campsite. Although surrounded with game-filled mountains, it offered protection from winter winds, a dependable water supply, and plenty of grass for grazing horses after they were procured. Great scars on some of the area's Ponderosa pines are said to have been created when Indians removed the bark for medicinal purposes. Archaeologists in search of prehistoric Ponil artifacts often encounter later Ute campsites, including crude pottery and well-defined tipi circles.

Marauders from the Plains

The Indians of the eastern plains were very different from the Utes and Jicarilla Apaches who resided in the mountains of western Colfax County. Including the Kiowa, Comanche, and sometimes other bands, these tribes were far less peaceful but much more colorful than their highland neighbors.

Typical flatland peoples, they depended on the buffalo to supply their daily needs. Clothing, shelter, food, tools, and even fuel were derived from the great shaggy beasts who frequented the plains, wandering as far west as the Moreno Valley and even north into Ponil Park. Because they were forced to migrate in search of the vital buffalo, the Plains people did not maintain permanent villages or practice agriculture.

Not until after they obtained horses from the Spaniards in the late 1600s, however, did they develop the spectacular characteristics for which they became known. Once an Indian had a swift mount, hunting buffalo became an exciting sport rather than a dreary necessity. The range of the nomads increased many times, and horse stealing became the chief occupation of every young man.

Raiding and warfare also became important once the Plainsmen were mounted. Almost as soon as they made contact, Comanche and Kiowa warriors attacked the peaceful Utes and Jicarillas, frequently driving them into a refuge high in the Sangre de

Comanche warrior "Horse Back" in camp. William Soule, 1873.

Library of Congress Prints and Photographs Division, Public Domain Images.

Cristo Mountains. Retaliatory attacks naturally followed, so that raids continued regularly for two hundred years.

War constituted an important spiritual activity for all participants. Elaborate religious preparations were undertaken before setting out on a raid, with special prayers, fasting, and symbolic body painting. Even in the heat of battle, ritual played an important role. "Counting coup" was practiced according to a prescribed procedure, while the bodies of those killed on either side would be scalped and mutilated.

The Indians neither gave nor expected to receive any leniency. Adult males were seldom captured, but those who were would await being tied to posts and murdered in the cruelest possible manner. Imprisoned children might be savagely mutilated, while enemy women would be abused by their captors and forced to perform the heaviest and most unpleasant work.

For every Indian warrior no death was as honorable as one secured during battle. A man who wished to sacrifice his life in battle signaled his intention by stripping himself naked before entering battle, where sure death would follow. Thereafter, however, great honor forever glorified his name.

Because the Plains Indians depended so heavily on the buffalo and were brave warriors, the conquest of northern New Mexico became immeasurable more difficult. From the Europeans' first arrival in the early 1700s until the 1870s they attempted, usually without success, to expel the warring tribes from Colfax County.

Plans for La Jicarilla

After nearly two hundred years of exploration and conquest, Europeans finally reached Colfax County in the early 1700s. They contacted the Indians in the region and even considered establishing permanent settlements, although such plans were soon abandoned.

Several reasons motivated Spain to move northward during these years. As part of their continuing expansion in Texas, California, and Arizona, this region marked a logical extension of their earlier efforts. They also hoped to put an end to Indian attacks which menaced the settled areas. Once the Pueblos had been subdued, they naturally turned their attention to the northern raiders. Finally, Spain feared the loss of the area to French rivals who were approaching it from the northeast. As rumors reached Mexico City that Louisiana traders were inching toward the southern Rockies, officials suddenly became interested in defending their previously neglected northern boundary.

A number of different expeditions visited the area in the early 18th century. Leading the first was Diego de Vargas, who was chasing Pueblo Indians who had escaped the reconquest. Some years later a Spanish captain named Ulibarri pursued renegades from Pecos Pueblo as far north as the Arkansas River, while a third man names Valverde followed in 1719.

Each of the conquerors visited an Apache settlement they named "La Jicarilla" which was probably located either on the Rayado or Cimarron Rivers near the base of the Sangre de Cristo Mountains. There they met with Indians who pleaded for protection from the hostile Plains tribes. Rumors of Frenchmen on the Arkansas River further persuaded them of the need to effectively control the region.

Elaborate plans were made for the settlement of La Jicarilla. The Indians would be allotted strips of land and taught how to cultivate it. They would be provided with axes and other tools so they could cut timber in the mountains for use in buildings throughout New Mexico. Valuable mines that were supposed to exist in the mountains might even be worked. Priests who were to move into the town could provide religious instruction, while some Spaniards might be persuaded to leave Santa Fe and settle there. A small garrison of troops would deter raiding Plains Indians and also defend the region against French incursion.

Spanish seat of government in Mexico City, founded in 1612,
as it appeared in the 1800s.

Library of Congress Prints and Photographs Division, Public Domain Images.

When the plan was submitted to officials in Mexico City, however, they were severely criticized. French interest in westward expansion seemed to be dwindling, so the Mexican territory was no longer considered threatened. Moreover, government leaders realized that it wold be impossible to accomplish their objectives without the expenditure of large amounts of money and the deployment of many troops. If the Indians wished to be safe from attack and to learn the ways of the Church, then they should move closer to already established settlements. It was more important to Spain to hold onto what she already had than to expand herself far into the frontier, weakening the entire imperial structure.

With the abandonment of plans to establish a Spanish town at La Jicarilla, European influence rapidly declined in northern New Mexico. Not until the early 1800s would a new group of invaders, this time from the United States, tramp through the wild Indian country.

America Moves West

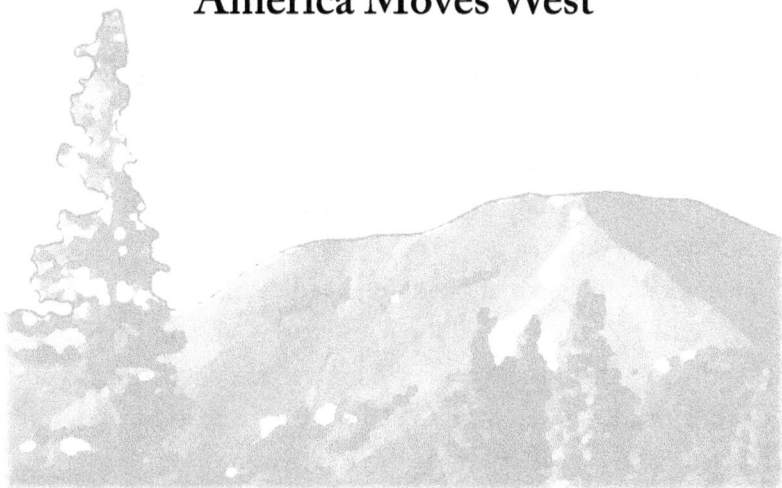

American Discovery of the Southwest

Although a handful of American and French trappers already had reached Santa Fe, few non-Mexicans probed the Southwest before the United States acquired Louisiana in 1803. As long as enfeebled Spain controlled the vast area west of the Mississippi, President Thomas Jefferson, like his two predecessors, devoted little attention to it. But in 1800 France secured possession of Louisiana and threatened to close the Mississippi River to Americans.

Then Jefferson acted. James Monroe and Robert Livingstone sailed to Paris ostensibly to purchase New Orleans, but they were able to buy not only the mouth of the Mississippi, but also the entire Louisiana Territory stretching westward to the Rocky Mountains. With the opportunity to nearly double the size of the country, Jefferson approved the extensive acquisition.

Plans immediately went forward to explore the new territory. While the more famous trek of Lewis and Clark was occurring in the north, several smaller and less successful expeditions were carried out in the south. To learn the vague boundaries of Louisiana and the nature of what he had acquired, Jefferson sent William Dunbar and George Hunter from Natchez, Mississippi, up the Washita River through what is today Arkansas in 1805. The following year Thomas Freeman led a second group 600 miles up the Red River until he met a contingent of Spanish soldiers and was forced to return.

Even before Freeman had returned, a far more important party led by Zebulon M. Pike had left the Missouri River. Successfully avoiding the Spaniards, he ventured up the Arkansas River, continuing westward to explore the "Mexican Mountains" in search of the headwaters of the Red River.

Soon the lieutenant encountered difficulties which plagued the remainder of the journey. Poorly prepared for winter, his men suffered from the extreme cold in Colorado. Then food supplies ran low. In desperation the party straggled into the San Luis Valley where they erected a stockade. But the Spanish appeared, placed the expedition under arrest, and marched them south to Santa Fe and eventually to Chihuahua City before they were escorted back to US territory.

Although often described as a failure and its leader criticized for losing his way, the Pike Expedition opened up the entire Southwest to the United States. His accurate reports of the Sangre de Cristo Mountains and the New Mexican settlements paved the way for many other American expeditions and the eventual opening of the Santa Fe Trail.

A less successful expedition soon followed under Major Stephen H. Long. Departing Nebraska in 1820, he reached the Rockies via the Platte River, continuing southward until he reached Pueblo, Colorado. Crossing the Purgatory River just

Spaniards escorting Zebulon Pike into Santa Fe, by Frederic Remington.
Library of Congress Prints and Photographs Division, Public Domain Images.

north of Raton Pass, he finally reached the Canadian River in eastern Colfax County and crossed through Union County on his way east to Arkansas.

Haphazardly organized and poorly directed, Long's party accomplished little in the way of exploring or mapping. Collecting a few botanical and geological specimens, they also climbed Pike's Peak for the first time. Long is best remembered for his description of the Great Plains, perhaps developed after wandering across eastern Colfax County. He wrote that the Great American Desert was "wholly unfit for cultivation and of course uninhabitable by a people depending upon agriculture for their subsistence." To his way of thinking, the region was valuable only as a "range for buffaloes, wild goats, and other wild game."

William Becknell: Pathfinder to Santa Fe

Often titled the "Founder of the Santa Fe trade and Father of the Santa Fe Trail," Captain William Becknell first learned of New Mexico's desire to trade in 1821. He advertised in the *Missouri Intelligencer* for men "to go westward for the purpose of trading for horses and mules and catching wild animals of every description." When the adventurers met some Mexicans near the Rockies, Becknell agreed to accompany them to Santa Fe. Easily disposing of their few trade goods, the men realized such handsome profits that they soon returned, and before long a lucrative trade blossomed between the United States and New Mexico.

In response to news of Becknell's initial success, seventy other traders carried nearly $15,000 in goods to New Mexico during 1822. Captain Benjamin Cooper left in mid-May and, although it was rumored that he had been "robbed by Indians and left in a starving condition," Cooper arrived in Santa Fe without incident. Instead of traversing Becknell's previous route south out of Colfax County, he apparently crossed the western mountains to Taos before turning south to the capital. No evidence indicates exactly where they traveled, but it is possible that they pulled their mules and horses up the Cimarron, Rayado, or Mora Canyons through the Sangre de Cristos.

Santa Fe wagon train crossing the prairie, by Frederic Remington.
Wikimedia Commons, California Historical Society Collection, CC3.0

Departing only a few days later, Becknell also blazed new trails that year. After reaching the upper Arkansas River, the party of thirty decided to avoid the treacherous Raton Pass by steering more directly for Santa Fe across the prairies. "With no other guide but the starry heavens," chronicler Josiah Gregg wrote, they "embarked upon the arid plains which extended far and wide before them to the Cimarron River."

Unable to procure water along the way, they nearly died. Forced finally to kill their dogs and cut the ears off their mules in hope of satisfying "their burning thirst with the hot blood," only the discovery of a lone buffalo fresh from a water hole saved the group. "The hapless intruder was immediately dispatched and invigorating draught procured from its stomach," Gregg reported, adding that one survivor told him "nothing ever passed his lips which gave him such exquisite delight as his first draught of that filthy beverage."

Successfully navigating what became the Dry Cimarron Branch of the trail, Becknell had opened a second route to Santa Fe. In later years it became increasingly popular as water holes were better known and Indian depredations decreased.

During his 1822 journey Becknell may have used the first wagons to carry freight across the Santa Fe Trail. Earlier traders using pack horses or mules had been limited in the amount and kind of goods they could haul. Originally designed by the Conestoga Wagon Works in Pennsylvania and later copied with alterations by several St. Louis manufacturers, the sway-backed wagons with their huge canopies to repel the sun and rain made it possible to transport larger quantities of merchandise across the plains. Because the wagons traveled slowly, however, many traders continued to rely on horses so they could reach the New Mexican markets sooner.

Westward Across the Plains

Tanned buckskin-clad drivers inspected every inch of their equipment to be sure that no spoke would crack, no strap break, no screw pull loose. Certain that every possible item had been crammed into their great wagons, packers roped down the loads, while local merchants stood by to fill any remaining space. Entrepreneurs in distinctive black attire whispered last-minute instructions to their representatives for avoiding duty fees and making the best deals in Santa Fe.

Mexicans who had herded mules, horses, or oxen from outlying pastures raced to harness their teams. Final farewells from tearful wives and excited children increased as the men moved to their places. Then from the front a call of "Ready?" rang out, and a hundred voices answered "All set!" With every wagon poised, the captain's cry of "Stretch out!" was blurred by the noises of barking dogs and shouting people. The Santa Fe caravan was heading west.

The sounds of a departing wagon train were heard in several frontier Missouri towns. Franklin gave birth to the trade and nurtured it for several seasons. Located just west of Franklin, Independence became the next point of embarkation for plains travelers. Other towns later vied for a role in the Mexican commerce. Westport and Kansas City grew and prospered during the early 1840s as traders took advantage of their location further west. The establishment of Fort Osage and Fort Leavenworth on either side of Kansas City lent a further advantage to the area. A few caravans which started from Little Rock, Arkansas, followed a southerly route through Texas to Santa Fe.

Normally the caravan left Missouri in the spring, sold during the summer in the Southwest, and returned by late fall. Leaving before the snows had melted on the plains was impossible, but too late a departure could mean encountering winter storms before reaching the settlements on the return trip.

Ox-drawn freight wagons approaching the foothills.
Library of Congress Prints and Photographs Division, Public Domain Images.

In reality, no marked trail stretched across the flatlands but caravan leaders explored their own routes along the river bottoms and across the grassy prairies. The need to find pasture for livestock frequently necessitated detours, as did avoiding the muddy ruts of a previous caravan. Often traveling two or even four abreast, a single caravan covered a span as wide as fifty yards. "One need only compare the various records to discover that the Santa Fe Trail was not a road nor even a trace," one recent historian has written, "but a series of tracks meandering over the plains in only the most general single course."

For nearly every caravan, the first important stop was Council Grove, one hundred and fifty miles or ten day's journey west of Independence. Although beautiful to see, traders kept busy making final preparations at the site before entering the wilderness to the west. Electing one of their members as caravan leader, the men also established regulations regarding the plan of travel, setting up camp, assigning sentries, and defending themselves against possible Indian attack.

West of Council Grove travelers entered the wilds. Only well-established campsites marked the route, for few landmarks broke the monotonous prairies which stretched for hundreds of miles in every direction. Boredom posed the greatest psychological problem, as man and beast alike tired of the dreary scenery and limited company. Nerves and tempers frequently frayed, but here too the real adventure began. Indians might appear at any time. What looked like a tree against the horizon might be a native scout, an antelope, or a buffalo—or maybe even the distant mountains.

Perils of the Santa Fe Trail

Anywhere west of Council Grove, traders were likely to encounter Indians, the most dramatic and frequently recorded kind of danger. Technically at peace after 1825, the eastern Osage tribe seldom disturbed merchants, but their western neighbors, the Pawnee, Comanche, and Kiowa, continually threatened war.

Travelers seldom recognized the natives' presence until a group of five to a dozen suddenly appeared from a nearby hill, riding rapidly toward the caravan. It was risky to attack an entire train, especially one guarded by soldiers, so the Indians normally conversed through signs for a few minutes while they appraised the party's strength. After such an Indian encounter the number of guards was doubled, and no one dared stray far from the wagons.

As early as 1822 Captain William Becknell told of eight men he had sent to recover some straying horses. Two of them spotted Indians, whom they tried to outrun. The natives soon overtook the pair, however, stripped them naked, administered a "barbarous whipping," and stole their mounts. Fortunately, the helpless men were luckier than many and were able to rejoin their party.

Four members of Captain Bennett Riley's military escort learned the danger of leaving the caravan during the 1829 trek. When their enlistments were up, they insisted on leaving the train midway across the plains to return to Missouri. Only eight or ten miles out of camp, about thirty Indians suddenly attacked them. An attempt to talk peace failed when one soldier was fatally

Wagon train attacked by hostile Indians on the prairie.
Library of Congress Prints and Photographs Division, Public Domain Images.

shot while trying to shake hands. The remainder removed their packs and prepared to defend themselves against the screaming attackers, who by then were riding rapidly around them. Slowly retreating toward their group's encampment, the survivors succeeded in killing one Indian before they were rescued by a search party.

Their efforts thus temporarily thwarted, the natives waited until Riley sent a party of men in search of their dead comrade before they attacked the entire caravan, driving off the livestock. In total, fifty-four oxen, twenty horses, and several mules were lost. The soldiers never located their companion's corpse, but the survivors now willingly agreed to remain with the escort until it returned from the Mexican border.

As they neared the Arkansas River, the leaders of each caravan had to decide between the two major routes. The longer one, probably used by the first few caravans and always the more popular, proceeded along the Arkansas River to the Bent brothers' famous fort near the present town of Las Animas, Colorado. From there they headed south over Raton Pass where they could follow the edge of the Sangre de Cristos through Colfax County toward Santa Fe. Although longer and more rugged, this road offered protection from Indians as well as a reliable water supply which appealed to many caravan leaders.

The second route had been blazed by William Becknell and was called the Dry Cimarron Branch. It departed from the Arkansas River in Kansas and headed directly across the arid plains of Texas and eastern New Mexico to Wagon Mound, New Mexico, where it rejoined the Mountain Branch. Although many who selected it suffered from a lack of water or fell victim to the Comanche or Kiowa who frequented the area, this route was faster and easier on the wagons than the more rugged mountain route.

The Last Miles to Santa Fe

Soon after crossing Raton Pass, caravans passed through the area which would eventually become Colfax County. Nothing distinguished the area from the hundreds of miles through which the wagons had passed, but early travelers were overjoyed to see the mountains, find plentiful supplies of wood, and rest beneath a shade tree along a cool Rocky Mountain stream. Frequently they recorded stops along the Ponil, Cimarron, Rayado, and Canadian Rivers.

The exact path of the road during those early days cannot be ascertained with any certainty, but several tracks now visible from the air indicate frequent use of the area fronting the Sangre de Cristo Mountains from Cimarron to Rayado, where the area's first permanent settlement was eventually established.

For some, the Cimarron area marked the point of departure from the regular Santa Fe route. While surveying the road in 1825, George Sibley noted a gap in the mountains through which a "trace" or primitive trail ran to Taos. Exactly what the surveyor was referring to is uncertain, but the Taos Trail evidently followed either Cimarron Canyon or Moras Canyon just south of Rayado.

Because Sibley reported that wagons could pass through the gap with "some labour," he probably did not mean the narrow and extremely rough Cimarron Canyon, which was not generally used until after prospectors discovered gold in the 1860s. A narrow dry stream bed winding to the rim of La Grulla Mesa, Moras Canyon was evidently used frequently by Taos travelers during the post-Mexican era, and it was probably the "gap" referred to by Sibley. Early trappers and traders hauled goods via this route directly to Taos, where they could be sold at the annual fairs or in American-owned stores. Those who used this trail might even reach Santa Fe before their fellows who traveled the longer route along the eastern side of the mountains.

Santa Fe traders found no permanent settlements in Colfax County before 1844, although there was one notable attempt

Woodcut engraving of a wagon train entering Santa Fe around 1841.
Wikimedia Commons, Public Domain Image.

to establish a ranch. In 1830 Samuel Chambers, a veteran Santa Fe trader and mountaineer, petitioned the Mexican government for permission to colonize the Ponil River area. Examining his request, the New Mexico Departmental Assembly noted that Indian hostilities in the area threatened anyone who might reside there. They decided that until sufficient military force could be secured to provide protection, no such ranches would be allowed along the northern frontier.

Another week's travel carried Santa Fe caravans from the Canadian River toward their destination. As they approached the capital, a sudden excitement swept through the party. Men dirty from months of travel now bathed, changed into their best clean shirts or put on Sunday suits, and glued their hair in place with bear grease. Wagoneers piled as many goods as possible into each wagon to reduce the per-wagon import duties, and then the caravan rolled down the last hill into the ancient city.

An unusual activity also characterized the normally quiet Mexican town when the annual wagon trains arrived. Cries of "los Americanos" and "los carros" ran through the narrow streets. Crowds of citizens flocked to stare at the newly-arrived gringos, most of whom stared back at the strange surroundings with equal interest. While their employees noted the loveliest señoritas and the liveliest dance halls, merchants wrangled with customs officials who appraised goods and exacted duties. At last the long trek was over.

Taming the Northern Frontier

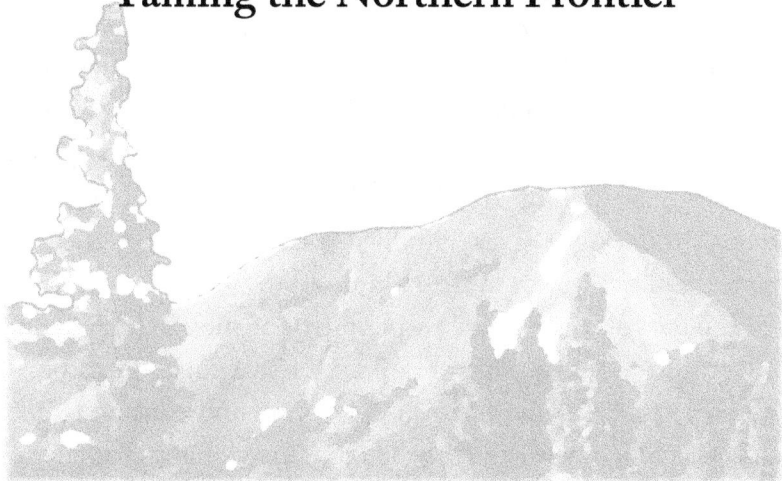

The Fur Trade

While Missouri merchants moved westward along the Santa Fe Trail, an equal number of easterners were exploring the mountains and valleys of the southern Rocky Mountains in search of beaver pelts. Like the traders, these men played a significant role in opening and developing the Southwest. Geographical exploration naturally resulted from their need to find new hunting grounds. Trails which they blazed across the American wilderness would eventually become the roads which carried wagon loads of pioneers and many of the mountaineers would themselves guide early expeditions.

The fur trade depended on the individual, rather than the company model that was the foundation of the Santa Fe trade. Because trapping was best accomplished by one or two men constantly moving across a geographic area, there were no permanent settlements that led to the development of towns and

39

cities. A solitary and temporary cabin far from anywhere was very typical.

Naturally, many of the finer qualities of civilization deteriorated under such conditions. Primitive but practical shelters and clothing set the beaver hunter apart from the merchant. Social customs practiced in the settlements meant little on the fringe of civilization where crude force usually predominated. The education of these western adventurers also fitted their occupation. Ciphering or writing counted for little, but the ability to read a moccasin track or beaver sign divided the skillful from the ignorant, the successful from the failures.

The area along the eastern periphery of the Rockies, including Colfax County, was one of the first regions where beaver were trapped. Despite Spanish opposition and constant Indian threats, Frenchmen evidently sought furs along the upper Canadian and Arkansas Rivers from the early nineteenth century. After the Louisiana Purchase, Americans joined them in greater numbers. August P. Choteau and Jules DeMun, arrested on the

Trappers' camp, Currier & Ives lithograph by Fanny Palmer, 1866.

Arkansas in 1815, had trapped in the area for over a year. Members of Joseph Philibert's party were reported to be trapping in northern New Mexico at the same time.

Early Santa Fe traders were often as interested in trapping beaver as in selling dry goods. Becknell, Cooper, and others carried traps and returned to the States with the pelts their men had secured. Jacob Fowler was returning from a beaver hunting expedition when he trekked through Colfax County's mountains in 1821.

By 1825, however, trapping parties were rapidly moving further westward into the heart of the Rockies. The number of beaver had been reduced to a point which prohibited profitable hunting. Because a single man needed to kill hundreds of animals annually, no area could long support extensive trapping. In addition, the Mexican government began to impose tighter restrictions on American fur seekers, forcing them away from the populated centers where their activities might be detected.

Although many trappers continued to bring pelts to the Bent brothers' Arkansas River fort, Taos, New Mexico, remained the center of the southwestern fur trade. This brought many men into the area who would later play significant parts in the development of the region. Besides the Bent brothers and Ceran St. Vrain, Antoine Robidoux, Old Bill Williams, Kit Carson, Dick Wootton, and Charles Beaubien originally came into the area in connection with the fur trade.

Charles Beaubien

No man may have contributed more to the early development of Colfax County and northeastern New Mexico than Charles Beaubien. Arriving from his native Canada soon after the opening of the Santa Fe Trail, Beaubien used a keen intellect and superior education to assume prominence in New Mexico. As fur trader, storekeeper, politician, judge, land developer, and comrade to many mountain men, he became wealthy and famous by 1846.

Beaubien subsequently aided in the establishment of American rule as United States federal judge, while simultaneously developing extensive land grants in southern Colorado and northern New Mexico. When he died in 1864, men throughout the territory lamented the passing of "an honored...and trusted man, friend, citizen, and patriot."

Beaubien spent his earliest years in an area far distant and vastly different from the Southwest. Born in October 1800 at Saint-Jean-Baptiste-de-Nicolet, Quebec, Canada, as a young man he began preparing to enter the priesthood. Attending the local seminary for eight years, he developed proficiency in Latin and a knowledge of the classics which would later set him apart from most of his unlearned associates. For unknown reasons, Beaubien decided to abandon church life. Unwilling to return home in disgrace, he apparently changed his given name from Alexis to Charles and departed for New Mexico.

Although during his initial years in the Southwest Beaubien apparently was involved in fur trading, he was never an enthusiastic outdoorsman and soon settled in Taos where he became an important supplier for the fur business. He fell in love and married Maria Paula Lobato, and from their union nine children were eventually born. Beaubien's influence in northern New Mexico increased rapidly. His business prospered as mountaineers sold him furs and purchased traps, foodstuffs, and the like. Known for an ability to evaluate pelts, the Taos storekeeper became one of the wealthiest residents in the area.

He also became a naturalized Mexican citizen in 1829 and began to assume importance in politics. An increasingly large group of non-Mexicans looked to him and his friend Charles Bent for leadership. Ceran St. Vrain, John Rowland, Stephen Louis Lee, and Antoine Leroux boasted of their friendship with

Portrait of Charles Beaubien.

Aztec Mill Collection, Cimarron,
New Mexico.

the merchant. But Beaubien often found himself in opposition to the political organization led by Father José Antonio Martínez. Ironically the two men had remarkably similar backgrounds and interests, but Martínez was extremely suspicious of foreigners, directing much of his antipathy toward the American Charles Bent and Canadian Beaubien.

New Mexico officials including Governor Manuel Armijo must have shared the clergyman's distrust. In an obvious effort to place the brunt of taxation on foreigners and naturalized Mexicans, in 1840 all native citizens were exempted from paying taxes on their storehouses and shops. In a further effort to drive their competitors out of business, informers were actively encouraged to report tax evaders. Provincial officials even raided the stores of Beaubien, Bent, and others in search of contraband.

Just as this anti-foreign sentiment was rising, Beaubien was preparing to acquire additional property in the northern wilderness of New Mexico. Anxious to achieve success, he looked for an influential partner to aid him. With the help of Governor

Armijo's Secretary, Guadalupe Miranda, he soon set out to acquire and settle what would eventually become Colfax County.

The Beaubien-Miranda Land Grant

By 1841 Charles Beaubien had decided to obtain a ranch on the eastern side of the Sangre de Cristo Mountains along the route of the Santa Fe Trail. There he could enlarge his already extensive holdings far from Father Martínez and the suspicious Mexican officials. He was sure that a store along the trail would be profitable, and the cattle and sheep raised there would build a proper estate for his many children.

But Beaubien was also certain that Governor Armijo would never grant such a tract to anyone of foreign birth. To influence the powerful governor, he invited Don Guadalupe Miranda to join him in the venture. As a distinguished Mexican citizen who had once superintended the Santa Fe public schools, Miranda could easily win the favor of Armijo and help obtain the desired property.

Beaubien and Miranda submitted their petition to the governor on January 8, 1841. They opened by describing the backward condition of the province: "With the possible exception of California," they explained, "New Mexico was the most retarded area of the country in intelligence, industry, and manufacturing." Yet it had all the natural advantages of abundant water, useful timber, fertile soil, and rich mineral deposits.

But for the want of enterprising men to exploit these features, the land was not being used. They felt that only by granting undeveloped tracts to private individuals could the country be made productive. Moreover, the territory was full of idle people who were a financial burden to the more industrious citizens, as well as being responsible for constant increases in crime. Put such unproductive hands to work, they urged, to improve the vacant land and develop New Mexico.

Despite the unpromising conditions they described, the two men believed that the future of the province was bright: "This is the age of progress and the march of intellect, and they are so rapid that we may expect, at a day not far distant, that they will reach even us." Turning to specifics, Beaubien and Miranda requested that they be granted a tract of land which they could improve by growing sugar beets or cotton and raising all kinds of livestock.

The boundaries they suggested were typically vague. The ranch would commence at the junction of the Cimarron and

Map showing the full extent of the Beaubien-Miranda Land Grant.

Aztec Mill Museum Collection, Cimarron, New Mexico.

Canadian Rivers, go north to the Una de Gato River, continue west across the summit of the mountains, turn south to the headwaters of the Rayado River, and then east to the starting point. Beaubien's partnership with Miranda was a prudent one, as Governor Armijo scrawled his approval on the margin of the petition several days later, authorizing the grantees to make the "proper use" of the land "which the law allows."

Unfortunately for Beaubien, within a few months violent anti-foreign sentiments were aroused throughout New Mexico by the arrival of the notorious Texas-Santa Fe expedition. Angry crowds milled in the streets of Santa Fe, threatening the life of any foreigner who dared to appear. In Taos, Beaubien's friend Charles Bent was arrested and carried off to the capital. This climate of unrest made it difficult for a man like Beaubien to establish settlements along the eastern edge of the mountains.

Not until February 12, 1843, did Beaubien and Miranda petition Taos Justice of the Peace Cornelio Vigil to put them in actual possession of their land. The official readily complied and ten days later accompanied them with five witnesses over the mountains to the land grant, where they erected a series of seven mounds to mark its boundaries.

"I took them by the hand," Vigil reported, "walked with them, caused them to throw earth, pull up weeds, and show other evidence of possession." After the ceremony concluded, Vigil declared them in "perfect and personal possession" of their ranch, guaranteeing that the grantees, their children, and successors should retain possession of the land forever.

Settling the Northern Frontier

Throughout 1843 and 1844 Beaubien and Miranda met constant opposition in their attempts to establish settlements on the land granted to them. To prevent Governor Armijo from hindering their plans, they apparently deeded him a one-fourth interest in the vast tract on March 2, 1843. From that day on, the governor always supported the owners against all attackers. More importantly, on that same day they negotiated an agreement with Charles Bent for the development of the area. In exchange for superintending future colonization activities, the experienced American entrepreneur whose Arkansas River fort had been so successful, was granted "the fourth part of the land which our possession includes."

As the landowners probably anticipated, the most intense opposition came from Father Martínez. Along with the chiefs of the Taos Pueblo, Martínez protested that the grant included part of the communal grazing and hunting lands reserved to the Pueblo. Moreover, he insisted that Charles Bent had an interest in the property and that the government of the Republic of Mexico could not give land to an unnaturalized foreigner. Although the grant was temporarily suspended while Armijo was out of office, the Departmental Assembly ruled in mid-April of 1844 that Martínez' claims were false and ordered that full use of the land be restored.

Almost immediately Beaubien and Bent moved ahead with their plans to establish settlements along the Ponil and Cimarron Rivers. Informed that a Justice of the Peace would be required in the area, the current governor, Felipe Sena, recommended Beaubien himself for the post in April 1844. A large number of people had already been offered land, no doubt on a share-crop basis, so that when the snows melted in the spring of 1844 several parties crossed the mountains from Taos to the grant.

One group under the leadership of Beaubien and Bent settled at a place called "El Ponil," where they built crude houses and planted corn or grain in the fertile valley. A second colony was established along the Cimarron River near where the village of Cimarron is now located. It was directed by Cornelio Vigil, who had earlier put the grantees in possession of their land. Before

47

long there were large fields of corn, beans, pumpkins, and the like in the area and several houses had been erected near the river.

The first two American settlers in the region were probably Kit Carson, already famous for his service as guide to John C. Fremont's first western expedition, and Richard Owens, who would soon make his own fame on a third Fremont trip. The two men decided they had "rambled enough" and in the spring of 1845 they settled along Cimarroncito Creek where they built a few small huts, put in at least fifteen acres of grain, and started cutting timber in order to make further improvements. In August Carson and Owens left the area to join Fremont, but the others apparently remained in the Cimarron Valley, continuing to cultivate its fertile soil.

North of the Cimarron, Tom Boggs and John Hatcher built cabins on the Ponil River during 1845 and were preparing to commence farming. The grizzly bears were so numerous that the men had to erect scaffolds in their fields from which to fight off

1921 Will James sketch of a grizzly foraging for food.

Library of Congress Prints and Photographs Division, Public Domain Images.

the savage beasts which ruined their crops and killed their livestock. Finally the pair decided that it was fruitless to raise corn and graze cattle in such an inhospitable area, so they abandoned their farm and returned to the relative safety of Bent's Fort.

Several factors contributed to the temporary abandonment of the Cimarron and Ponil areas. Constant Indian depredations, along with the harsh climate and primitive conditions, discouraged many of the settlers. Many Mexican officials continued to raise legal obstacles to development, while the arrival of the US Army in 1846 and the subsequent Taos uprising forced the remaining colonists to retreat to the security of the larger cities. However, shortly there would be a new colony on the Rayado River that would bring renewed life to the Beaubien-Miranda Grant.

A Permanent Colony on the Grant

Years of Decision and Change

Dramatic changes during the late 1840s hindered Charles Beaubien's plans for settling his New Mexican land grant. Most important in altering Beaubien's efforts was the arrival of American troops in New Mexico. Leaving Fort Leavenworth, Kansas, on June 26, 1846, General Stephen W. Kearney soon had 3,000 men on their way west. By the end of July soldiers began to arrive at Bent's Fort, which soon resembled an armed fortress. Advance parties headed south to scout the enemy positions, and in early August the main army began to march to the edge of the Sangre de Cristo Mountains.

Word of the approaching troops sent colonists fleeing from Beaubien's lands. When the soldiers reached the Ponil area they took over the ranch and its cattle, together with the less developed settlements on the Cimarron and Vermejo Rivers. In the months that followed, Americans passing through the area often used abandoned ranches in Colfax County as campgrounds and pastures for their livestock.

Normal business along the Santa Fe Trail halted. Except for a few herders who stayed along the Vermejo, Ponil, and Cimarron, there was no ranching activity. Certainly no large-scale attempt could be made toward colonization during a foreign invasion. Once Kearney had captured Santa Fe and transformed New Mexico into an American territory, the most prominent men assumed new roles as political officials. Charles Bent was selected to be the first American governor, while Beaubien served as one of three district judges in the new legal system.

Even more important than the United States' takeover, however, was the Taos uprising of January 1847. Often attributed to the Mexican nationalism of Father Martínez, the revolt was a last futile attempt by native New Mexicans and Pueblo Indians to overthrow the American regime. Sweeping through Taos in a

Engraving of General Kearney at the plaza in Las Vegas, proclaiming New Mexico part of the United States on August 15, 1846.

Wikimedia Commons Public Domain Image.

reign of terror not unlike that of the French Revolution, frenzied mobs struck down everyone who had opposed them.

Fortunately, Charles Beaubien was holding court in Rio Arriba County, thus being spared from the bloodshed. Others involved in the early settlement of Colfax County were less fortunate. Attackers rushed into Governor Bent's home, murdering and scalping the official while his family frantically fled through a hole they dug through an adobe wall. Cornelio Vigil, who had confirmed the grant and helped settle Cimarron, was caught and cruelly butchered. A native woman pointed out Beaubien's son, Narciso, who had hidden with a friend under a hay stack. Quickly discovered, they suffered death at the hands of the mob.

These events naturally affected the course of Colfax County's development. Deprived of his son and those men who had helped with earlier settlement, Charles Beaubien now recruited new colonizers. The most important would be his two sons-in-law, Jesus G. Abreu, who had married his daughter Petra, and Lucien B. Maxwell who was the husband of his daughter Luz. Joined by an old family friend, Joseph Pley, these men would soon venture across the mountains to start a new settlement, this time along the banks of the Rayado River on the southern portion of the grant.

The Rise of Lucien Maxwell

Although his importance has often been exaggerated even to the point of overshadowing his far more significant father-in-law, Lucien Bonaparte Maxwell was surely one of the most colorful figures involved in the early settlement of Colfax County. Semiliterate and rough around the edges, Maxwell took advantage of several opportunities to reap fame and fortune in northern New Mexico. Yet an aura of drama, romance, and mystery which still surrounds his life has led most people to view the entire region as the "Kingdom of L.B. Maxwell."

Like Beaubien, Maxwell was raised in an atmosphere far removed and far different from the New Mexico wilderness. Born in September 1818 at Kaskaskia, Illinois, Lucien was the eldest son of Hugh H. Maxwell and Marie Odelle Maxwell. When he was only fifteen his father died in an accident, so young Maxwell moved into the mansion of his grandfather, Pierre Menard. A prominent Illinois politician, Menard served as his state's first Lieutenant Governor. Today a statue of him graces the state capital at Springfield, while an Illinois county is also named in his honor.

Young Maxwell received some education, but books did not interest him. Instead he dreamed of the out-of-doors and the great West he so often heard about from visiting frontiersmen. Soon he left the Menard home to join John Jacob Astor's American Fur Company, where he received an education in the ways of the woodsman and the trapper.

In 1842 Maxwell was employed as a hunter with the exploring expedition of "Pathfinder" John C. Fremont. Although his hunting abilities were often compared unfavorably to the more experienced guide Kit Carson, Maxwell did acquire an admirable reputation among his comrades and also became a close friend of Carson in the course of their western travels.

Evidently through Carson, Maxwell gained the acquaintance of the influential Beaubien family. On March 27, 1842, Lucien married the oldest Beaubien daughter, Luz, who was in her early teens. During the years that followed Maxwell traveled throughout the region carrying messages or supplies, trapping and hunting for Beaubien, the Bents, St. Vrain, Fremont, and others. For a time he even opened a Taos store with another frontiersman, James H. Quinn.

Just as Beaubien renewed his plans to establish permanent ranches on his land grant, Maxwell and Carson were looking for a new place to settle. As Carson later recalled: "We had been

Artist's conception
of Lucien Maxwell.

Aztec Mill Museum
Collection, Cimarron,
New Mexico.

leading a roving life long enough and now was the time, if ever, to make a home for ourselves and our children. We were getting old and could not expect to remain any length of time able to gain a livelihood as we had been [for] such a number of years." Together they moved across the mountains sometime during the spring of 1849.

Accompanying Maxwell and equal if not superior to him in authority, Beaubien sent Joseph Pley, a Spaniard who had prospered in business with St. Vrain and others at Mora. The grant owner no doubt thought that Maxwell and Carson could repel Indian attacks and overcome other frontier hardships, while Pley could more effectively manage the business end of the ranch and store which would be established. The site chosen for the new colony, which would be the first permanently planted in Colfax County, was Rayado, some eleven miles south of Cimarron along the edge of the Sangre de Cristos.

Settlement on the Rayado

Almost from the moment of its inception, Beaubien's Rayado colony prospered far more than had his earlier settlements. Not that the lands were more fertile or the colonizers more able, but the American government encouraged settlements, whereas the Mexicans had opposed them. Soldiers were now available to chastise the Indians, at the same time offering lucrative feed contracts to lure successful farmers. In short, Colfax County was slowly being tamed, making it less hazardous to live in the area as the years passed.

Within a few weeks after moving across the mountains, Beaubien's emissaries had selected a site along the Rayado River and began building and improving nearby property. Carson reported that they were "in a way of becoming prosperous." Driving an initial herd of livestock from Taos, the men were soon putting sheep, horses, cattle, and mules out to pasture in the nearby meadows. Four new men came to start other farms along the river that first spring, and fifteen more families joined them in 1850. Most worked on shares, with Beaubien providing land and supplies in exchange for part of the crop. Other Spanish-Americans were busy cutting timber, hauling it to the settlement, and sawing it into boards.

By the time Charles E. Pancoast, a Pennsylvanian headed for the California gold fields, reached Rayado on July 26, 1849, the settlement presented a formidable appearance. He wrote:

> On the 26th we crossed a mountain ridge and entered a beautiful valley covered with fine grass, over which herds of horses, cattle, and sheep were ranging; and about sundown we had the pleasure of seeing a Spanish rancho at the foot of a high mountain. This was Riadjo [sic], the rancho of the famous mountaineer Kit Carson, so long the scout and guide of General Fremont.

Lucien Maxwell's Rayado ranch house as it appears today.
National Scouting Museum Collection, Cimarron, New Mexico.

"The ranch house," Pancoast continued, "could not be said to be stylish. It was a two-story log affair, surrounded by adobe walls for purposes of fortification. Inside the wall were several adobe houses, and outside a number more, as well as a large corral and several buildings used as stables, slaughter houses, etc." A dozen or more Americans, Mexicans, and even Indians were to be observed in the area where all were fed at a single table, Pancoast reported. "Judging from the waste we saw," he added, "the table was of no mean order."

The most interesting part of the visit was an evening meeting with Kit Carson. Dressed "in first-class Indian style in buckskin coat and pants trimmed with leather doggles" and wearing a Mexican sombrero, the famous Westerner entertained them until eleven o'clock with stories of adventure and danger. Carson explained that great difficulties had been experienced in keeping the settlement safe from Indian attack, and now Kit hoped the Indians would behave. Yet it was still necessary to keep constant watch over the livestock.

Carson did not stay long at Rayado because a new call from Fremont drew him away to explore, leaving his wife and child at the ranch. In all spending less than eighteen months at the settlement, Carson did play an important role in pacifying the area, and today a museum on the site of his primitive adobe home plays proper homage to his work.

Indian Raids at Rayado

Without doubt the greatest danger to Beaubien's settlement at Rayado came from hostile Indians. Just as they had traditionally raided the Utes and Apaches in northeastern New Mexico, the Comanches and Kiowas now turned their attention to the newly-arrived settlement. As Carson had mentioned, livestock was their favorite prey. Occasionally a herder was killed, keeping the settlers in constant apprehension that an attempt would be made to drive them out of the region.

Early one morning when most of the men were gone, a German boy working at the ranch came running from the creek where he had been getting water, reporting that Indians were gathered on the hill for an attack. Soon a large party approached the gate demanding food and threatening hostilities if it was not provided. The wife of Tom Boggs, the famed mountain man, was staying at the ranch and recommended that rather than try to repel the natives, they should give them a feast—while one rider should be sent south toward Fort Union to get troops. Teresina Bent later recalled what followed:

So we women all set to work cooking coffee and meat and whatever else we had. I was twelve years old and the chief of the war party saw me and wanted to buy me to make me his wife. He kept offering horses...ten, fifteen, twenty horses. Mr. Boggs said for us to act friendly with the Indians and not make the chief angry. I was so frightened! And while I carried platters of food from the kitchen the tears were running down my cheeks. This made the chief laugh. He was bound to buy me, and when they all got through eating he said that they would wait. If I was not delivered to him by the time the sun touched a hill there in the west he would take me by force.

As Teresina waited nervously, the Indians camped outside waiting for the sun to set. Inside the adobe enclosure everyone scurried to take bullets to the men who were preparing for a fight. But just as the moment of the attack approached, Kit Carson and a company of soldiers rode dramatically up the road. The Indians fled, and Teresina said, "I was so glad because I did not want to go with the dirty chief."

A similar, although perhaps legendary, incident gained fame for Vidal Trujillo who had married Beaubien's daughter Leonora and moved to Rayado. One morning a party of Apache warriors appeared on the ridge north of the river. A fight seemed inevitable when two men sent out to see what they wanted were fired upon. As the men turned to flee, 600 warriors topped the hill and pursued the pair until they were inside the compound.

Conditions were especially bad since most of the men were gone and the ammunition supplies had run low. Trujillo knew that someone would have to ride for troops, so he volunteered. The mount he chose was *Rayado*, a fine racehorse named for the settlement. Once mounted and ready, the gates were thrown open and out sped the horse and rider. A later writer recalled:

Like a thunderbolt the big chestnut horse shot into the midst of the circling savages. Crouched low over his withers, Vidal,

Dragoons in a running battle with hostile Indians attempting to
steal livestock, by Frederic Remington.

Library of Congress Prints and Photographs Division, Public Domain Images.

a professional jockey, guided him through the savages in the
greatest race of his career. So unexpected the act and so complete the surprise, the flying rider was through the line before
the Indians knew what was happening....Fate rode with Vidal
Trujillo that day. Miraculously he escaped their missiles and
by virtue of the great horse under him, outran them.

Never daring to spare his horse, Trujillo pushed on as rapidly as possible until he reached Fort Union. There *Rayado*, his
last energy spent, fell dead. But the soldiers received the message
and departed northward, driving away the attackers. Once again
Rayado was secure.

Post Rayado

Realizing the necessity of having troops to protect the settlers, plans were soon initiated to station soldiers at the site. As a
result of the bloody massacre of J.M. White's party late in 1849,

Major William N. Grier apparently sent dragoons from Taos the following winter. Their commander was Sergeant William C. Holbrook. Soon the soldiers learned that Apache, Ute, and perhaps other bands were gathering near Rayado "meditating some bold and daring movement, or concerting schemes for spring outrages."

Early in April 1850 the anticipated attack came when the Indians swept down on a rancho two miles from Rayado, driving off the livestock and wounding two herders. Joined by Kit Carson and three other Americans from Rayado, Holbrook and his men hurried in pursuit. Locating the trail of the stolen animals which they followed for twenty-five miles, they finally came upon the attackers. Immediately Carson led an attack which killed five Indians and recaptured the stolen livestock. The men returned to Rayado taking the scalps with them as evidence of the great victory.

Major Grier wrote to congratulate the party on its success, declaring the expedition "a very handsome one and very creditable to the sergeant and his men." Less pleased at the report of soldiers having scalped Indians, he ordered Holbrook to say that the hair had been lifted by Mexican herders who arrived after the fight.

Having demonstrated the value of the troops, the Army issued orders on May 24, 1850, establishing a permanent military post at Rayado. About forty men from Companies G & I of the 2nd Dragoons were moved from Taos under the leadership of Grier to take up residence, initially staying in tents pitched near the Rayado compound. Maxwell had already begun to build a large house for himself, and he agreed to rent it to the government for $200 per month. Although displeased with the high cost, Grier knew it was the only accommodation available. Soldiers were soon put to work cutting timber to aid in completing their barracks.

Cavalrymen cooking breakfast at their encampment on the plains,
by Frederic Remington.

The only description of the short-lived post comes from Inspector General George A. McCall who visited Rayado on September 16, 1850. Generally pleased with what he saw, McCall
reported that Grier had "discharged his duties with zeal and
ability." However, he criticized the poor performance of the soldiers during a drill demonstration. The soldiers had been busy
moving their post, building their quarters, and chasing Indians
rather than practicing drills. McCall wrote: "They are not well-
instructed in the prescribed drill. Their appearance is that becoming hard service rather than parade duty."

As for the location, McCall proclaimed it "in every respect
a most eligible site for a frontier post." Near the Indians' home
territory, it was still close enough to a settlement where supplies
and forage could be obtained. Nearby wood supplies were excellent, the climate was even better than that of Santa Fe, allowing

easy movement of troops at any time of year. He suggested that a permanent fort built of adobe might well be erected on the site.

Following up on McCall's recommendations, Lieutenant John G. Parke, later famous for surveying a railroad route across Arizona, was ordered to make a thorough examination of the Rayado area to recommend the best site for a permanent post. Besides the availability of wood, water, forage, and food supplies for the garrison, his orders told him to evaluate the ability of troops to operate "to the most advantage over the greatest area of country and on the essential parts in the most prudent and effective manner."

Parke's report did not favor Rayado. On all sides of the settlement he found piñon-covered mesas which offered excellent cover for Indians, besides allowing the garrison "an exceedingly limited view" of the surrounding countryside. As an alternative he preferred the low mesa between Cimarron and Ponil ten miles to the north. Not only could soldiers there observe a larger area, but better grass and timber would provide additional advantages.

But the Army soon decided to ignore the Cimarron location, centering all of New Mexico's military forces at Fort Union to the south. On July 25, 1851, Col. E.V. Sumner commanding the District of New Mexico, ordered Captain Richard S. Ewell—later a famous Confederate general—to abandon the Rayado post. Maxwell pleaded that since he had agreed to help the Army scout a new trail to Fort Leavenworth, a detail of soldiers should be left. Fifteen men did remain for a short time, but on August 31, 1851, Post Rayado's short existence came to an end.

The Move to Cimarron

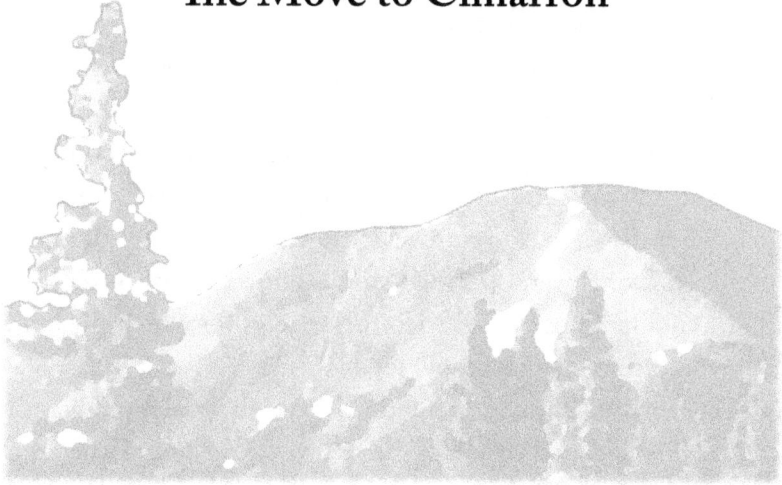

Maxwell on the Cimarron

By 1857 Lucien B. Maxwell was ready to leave the Rayado and strike out on his own. For nearly a decade he had managed the Beaubien ranch from which his father-in-law was profiting. But now the eastern New Mexico frontier was rapidly being pacified. The presence of troops had attracted a growing number of settlers, substantially reducing the Indian menace and making it safe for others to establish ranches in the region.

Maxwell selected a spot along the Cimarron River some three miles below the mouth of its rugged canyon as the site for his new settlement. Military reports indicated the defensive superiority of that location, and the valley around it provided plenty of clear water and abundant rich soil to carry out successful agricultural endeavors.

In addition, Maxwell's site was near the intersection of the Bent's Fort road and the still undeveloped Cimarron Canyon route to Taos. A store there would surely be even more profitable than the one at Rayado. Soon Maxwell moved to the Cimarron, and before long he had crews of men building his ranch headquarters there.

The buildings erected along the Cimarron that first year were perhaps indicative of the expansive plans which Maxwell already had for the ranch. Built of adobe, the house consisted of a pair of large two-story wings which faced onto a central courtyard. Like the Rayado compound, Maxwell's home was surrounded by massive walls to exclude unwelcome visitors. Inside, the neatly plastered rooms were spacious, but as one early visitor reported, they contained none of the rich furnishings for which the building would someday be renowned.

One early visitor commented, "The room we slept in was carpeted, but had not even a chair. However, in one corner there was a pile of wool mattresses and bedding from which the servants made beds for us on the floor at night. So far as we saw, there was only one room in the house that had a bedstead, and that was the one occupied by Maxwell and his wife." Following Mexican custom, there were separate dining rooms in the house for men and women. Because of the large number of visitors and employees that were already flocking to the Cimarron, the men's dining room was large enough to seat at least twenty people.

From Maxwell's residence one could see the great herds of cattle and flocks of sheep which were grazing on the ranch. Closer in were large fields of grain and corn cultivated on shares by farmers who had moved up from the Rayado or across the mountains from Taos. A store building, blacksmith shop, barns, and countless small adobe huts where farmers and laborers lived encircled the ranch house. Maxwell was soon beginning to talk of a huge stone grist mill where he could grind his own meal, thus saving the expensive trip across the mountains.

Lucien Maxwell's Cimarron Ranch, by Manville Chapman.
Aztec Mill Museum Collection, Cimarron, New Mexico.

"The surroundings and whole atmosphere of the place," wrote an early chronicler, "reminded me of the descriptions I had read of baronial estates in Europe." Maxwell's position was further improved when he secured Miranda's share of the grant. Because of financial difficulties, the Mexican—who had fled south at the time of the American invasion—wrote his partner Beaubien in 1858 expressing a desire to sell his interest. Beaubien did not wish to acquire Miranda's share, but his energetic son-in-law was very interested. On April 7, 1858, Miranda's son Pablo sold his father's interest in the property to Maxwell for $2,500.

Maxwell still did not possess clear title to the land where his adobe mansion had been erected. On September 14, 1858, he purchased the Beaubien share of the tract extending for over two miles in each direction from his Cimarron home for $500. What would someday become the village of Cimarron was now known as "Maxwell's Ranch."

Soon after these land purchases had been completed, Maxwell began his largest construction project to date. Under the supervision of millwright R.M. Blackmore, men were soon at work building a three-story stone grist mill several hundred yards from the Maxwell home. Powered by water from the Cimarron River, the mill would produce three hundred sacks of flour each day. Completion of the project was initially announced for November 1861, although it was apparently not finished for three years. By then, however, the demand for milled products had greatly increased, for Cimarron had been selected as the site of an Indian Agency, and Lucien Maxwell had acquired a contract to feed the natives.

The Cimarron Indian Agency

Few events were as significant in the long-range development of Colfax County as the establishment of a US government Indian Agency at Cimarron in 1861. For one thing, the Indians would henceforth be fed by the government, lessening the likelihood of their raiding nearby ranchers. More important still, large sums of money would be spent by government officials to

Maxwell's grist mill with Indians receiving rations, about 1870.

Aztec Mill Museum Collection, Cimarron, New Mexico.

provide food for the Indians. For the first time, a ready motive would induce settlers to grow grain and raise cattle for sale.

Originally the agency had been located in Taos, but by 1861 the increasing population made the town undesirable as a location for the Utes and Jicarilla Apaches. The local stills produced too much "Taos Lightning" to which the natives became addicted, and once they were full of the potent liquor even Indian agent Kit Carson could not control them. In June 1861 when Carson resigned his post as Indian agent to join the US Army and fight for the preservation of the Union, government officials decided to move the 1,500 Indians into a more remote region. Perhaps influenced by Maxwell, who realized the advantages of having the agency located at his ranch, politicians selected Cimarron as the site.

The first Cimarron agent was William F.M. Arny, an idealistic Kansan inspired by religious reformer Alexander Campbell, the founder of the Disciples of Christ. Arny had gained experience during the struggle over the spread of slavery into the West, and he was now eager to tackle his new assignment ministering to the Indians.

Shortly after his arrival the agent proposed an elaborate program for the education and civilization of his charges. Because no facilities were available at Maxwell's, he pleaded for the buildings he thought necessary to meet his lofty goals. The "sole hope for the improvement and elevation" of the red man was the education of native children. A "taste for civilized life" must be created among the young Indians before the unsavory habits of the tribe could be altered. Cimarron, Arny wrote, was the ideal location for an industrial and agricultural school for these Indians. Rich soil and adequate water could produce many varieties of vegetables and grains to feed the natives, with few Americans or Mexicans to corrupt them.

No doubt encouraged by Maxwell, who could visualize liberal federal appropriations pouring into his coffers, Agent Arny suggested that as a first step the government negotiate a new treaty with the Utes and Apaches. The Indian Bureau, he thought, should provide them with clothing and tools for farming, but all Indian children aged eight to sixteen should be turned over to the agent who would clothe, feed, and educate them. While these native scholars learned to read and write, they would also devote three hours every day to laboring in the fields.

In March 1862 the idealistic plans of the agent took concrete form when Arny leased 1,280 acres in Ponil Canyon just north of Cimarron from Lucien Maxwell for twenty dollars per year. Shortly the founder of Cimarron was also selling flour and beef to the agency at high prices.

Soon, however, serious problems arose which threatened the existence not only of the Indian Agency but of the Cimarron settlement itself. First, New Mexico was invaded by Confederate troops from Texas. After the inglorious surrenders in the southern part of the territory, the Texans marched north through Santa Fe, threatening to claim the territory for the South everywhere they went.

Cimarron Indian Agency ration tokens unearthed in Ponil Canyon
during an archaeological dig in the 1970s.

David T. Kirkpatrick Collection.

Maxwell took advantage of food shortages resulting from the invasion and abruptly raised the price of foodstuffs sold to the government. Arny, supplied with insufficient funds to buy corn and wheat for his charges, feared that they would either starve to death or provoke a war with the settlers by stealing their livestock. To further disturb matters, a smallpox epidemic broke out among the Indians, killing seventeen within a few days.

While war threatened, Arny attempted to develop an agency on the Ponil where the Indians could grow their own food, freeing them from dependence on Maxwell. Offices, schoolrooms, a kitchen, and council room, plus quarters for the agent, were soon completed. A corral was built to hold horses and cattle, and an adjoining plot would become the vegetable garden by the next spring.

With Arny's appointment as Territorial Secretary the following year, many of his plans were forgotten. Although the Confederates were at last ousted and the smallpox eradicated, constant friction between Indians and local settlers would continue for another fifteen years.

The Ute and Jicarilla Agency: 1862-67

The optimistic plans which Agent Arny had for the Cimarron agency soon faded into the background. Arny himself became Territorial Secretary in 1862, moving south to Santa Fe. In his place came Levi J. Keithly, "a plain, honest, straightforward old farmer." Lacking any of the idealism and reforming spirit which had characterized his predecessor, the new agent believed that the Indians were "devoid of anything like generosity, honesty, or good faith." Instead of opening schools and teaching them to farm, he accused them of attacking livestock and urged that they be confined on a reservation policed by armed troops. Abandoning the agency that Arny had erected on the Ponil, he moved his headquarters back to Cimarron where buildings were rented from Lucien Maxwell.

Simultaneously, complaints of Indian depredations on nearby farms began to increase. Samuel B. Watrous, a pioneering Sapello River rancher for whom a town is now named, was especially vocal. All of Arny's talk was "transparent humbug," he insisted, predicting that an Indian uprising would soon occur. When that bloody day came, the responsibility must rest upon the shoulders of those like Arny who had "fastened this scourge upon us and sustained their action by the aid of forgery and lies."

As if such attacks were insufficient, Cimarron residents seemed just as willing to sell whiskey to the Indians as had their neighbors in Taos. Any Indian with money could obtain the fiery liquid from any one of a dozen places in the little village. Keithly also reported that the Indians had developed such a taste for liquor that they would sell all their possessions for it. Even the corn they grew was turned into a "kind of beer which they

1875 *Harper's Weekly* engraving showing Indians
receiving rations at an Indian Agency.

Library of Congress Prints and Photographs Division, Public Domain Images.

drink day and night to excess, regardless of the wants of wife and child."

Nor were troubles limited to the Utes and Jicarillas. Late in August 1863 a party of Arapahoes and Cheyennes visited the settlement, leaving with a herd of Ute horses. Eager for revenge, the Moaches chased after the thieves. Although unsuccessful in recovering their livestock, the natives did kill one Cheyenne whose scalp they joyfully paraded through Cimarron.

A second raid from the Plains cost Maxwell forty mares, and the third time marauders visited Cimarron they surrounded the agency, demanding to know where the Utes were camped. Thus warned of the impending attack, the Cimarron Indians took the offensive and chased their historic enemies back toward the east. In the skirmish which followed, one Arapaho was killed and a Ute wounded.

Such difficult conditions would worsen, however, before they improved. A nation at war to preserve its very existence could send only the least competent officials for the Indian service, and a series of corrupt, worthless agents would succeed Keithly. It was much more important to spend limited funds to buy uniforms and guns for Union soldiers than blankets and corn for southwestern savages. Time after time when money did not arrive from Washington or Santa Fe, Maxwell fed the Indians out of his own pocket. If he ever refused, hunger pains would surely cause an Indian outbreak.

Moreover, as Cimarron's population grew, conditions deteriorated for the natives. The hunting and camping areas where they had lived and secured food for hundreds of years were now being used by farmers and ranchers. The deer which they desperately needed for food and clothing almost disappeared. No longer could the Indians venture out onto the plains in search of buffalo.

To add to the belligerency of the natives, liquor sales constantly increased. While they were on drunken binges, even the most reliable and friendly Indians might let their suppressed hatreds overflow. Occasional attacks on farmers and citizens threatened to provoke an all-out war. But until 1867 at least the Army, the agents, and especially Lucien Maxwell had prevented the often predicted bloodbath. The sudden population explosion caused by the discovery of gold in the area, however, would make it even more difficult to keep the peace.

The Discovery of Gold

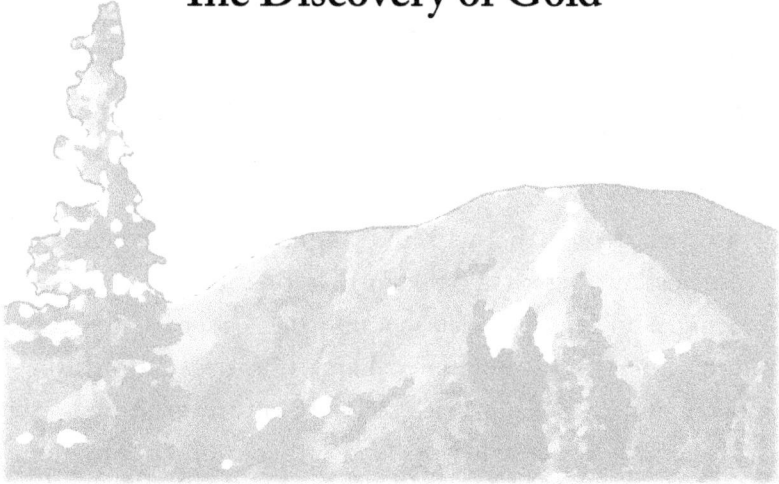

Gold on Baldy Mountain

Rumors had long circulated that there was gold hidden in the Sangre de Cristo Mountains west of Cimarron. After all, early visitors may have reasoned, because large deposits had been discovered to the south near Santa Fe and much grander ones in Colorado to the north, it seemed logical that some must also be found in between.

A series of dramatic events culminating in a full-scale gold rush at Cimarron began in the late summer of 1866. Eager to trade anything they could find for food or liquor, a party of Utes and Jicarillas had found a hillside on Baldy Mountain covered with colorful lumps of azurite, a high-grade copper ore. Returning to Cimarron with their "pretty rock," the natives traded it to a group of Fort Union soldiers who were at Maxwell's ranch to investigate Indian attacks on livestock. With the Civil War over, these men probably realized that they would shortly be mustered out of the service, and a copper mine could make them rich.

William H. Moore, a Fort Union sutler, and others paid the Indians for their rock and sent one man back with a native guide to locate the source of the copper. The pair climbed nearly to the top of Baldy Mountain before they found the slope, thickly blanketed with the greenish float. The man laid out a claim, known afterward as the "Copper Mine" or "Mystic Lode," jotted down its location, and raced back to tell Moore and the others of his exciting find.

This report, together with the samples of float brought down to the post, further excited the Fort Union men. Moore, William Kroenig, and several others became the leaders of the copper mining interests. They ordered Larry Bronson, Pete Kinsinger, and a man named Kelley back to Baldy in October 1866 to start the necessary assessment work and to begin uncovering ore for shipment.

Leaving the fort one morning, the three traveled to Cimarron, continued west through the narrow Cimarron Canyon, and turned into the Moreno Valley. From there they climbed north

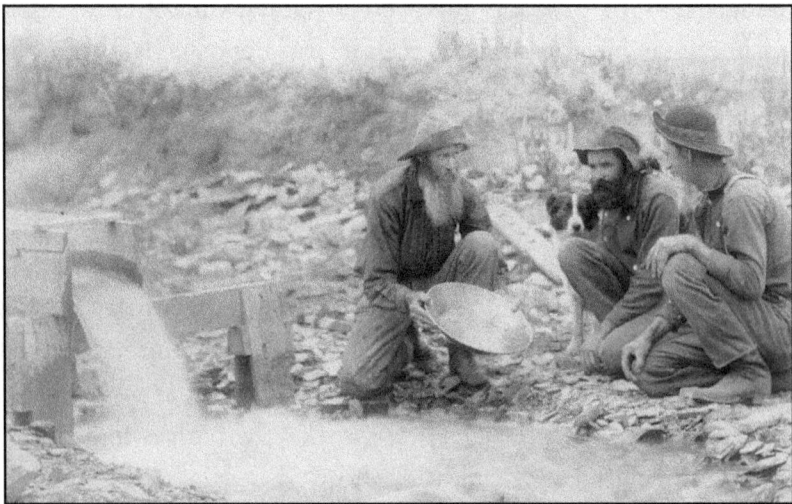

The first prospectors panned for gold along streams.
Library of Congress Prints and Photographs Division, Public Domain Images.

up Willow Creek, the southernmost stream flowing off the west side of Baldy. It was late afternoon when they arrived near the top. Rather than start work so late in the day, the men decided to set up camp and spend the night. Bronson and Kinsinger cooked supper while Kelley took a gold pan from his pack and casually washed some creek gravel in it. Before long he ran to the cooks, showing them the gold flakes he had found in the pan.

All supper plans were abandoned as the trio picked up tools and set to work in the stream. Thoughts of a copper bonanza were forgotten during the next few days as the three explored their private gold field, digging exploratory trenches, working gravel beds, and chipping away at likely-looking rocks. Since they knew it was too late in the season for extensive operations, each swore to say nothing of the discovery until spring when they expected to return to a carefully marked tree under which they had camped, lay out claims, and make themselves rich. Retreating from the mountains late in the fall of 1866, they were certain of the riches beneath them. There was gold on Baldy Mountain.

The three discoverers, seething with excitement over their find, could never have kept such a secret. Within weeks after their return everyone at the fort had heard the story. Some especially anxious men may even have left the fort, spending the winter prospecting and mining in the snow-covered mountains. Hundreds more saw the coarse gold flakes taken from Baldy, each telling a few close friends, until the southern Rockies echoed with news of the gold strike on the Maxwell Grant.

By 1867 the Colorado gold rush had collapsed. Thousands of Pike's Peak miners making unsatisfactory returns from poor claims, and unable to find work, were ready to move on. Many packed their shovels and pans and headed south. Uncle Dick Wootton, whose toll gate in Raton Pass blocked the path, graciously collected fees from the miners who tramped toward Cimarron.

By early June three hundred men had left their posts at Fort Union to head for the gold fields. Miners had crowded around Maxwell's mansion even before the snows stopped falling. With the first warm rays of the spring sun, they flooded the new El Dorado, taking up claims and washing out gold. Surely, declared one miner, northern New Mexico would be "another California."

Retrieving Aztec Riches

Just as before in California and Colorado, the earliest Moreno Valley mining methods were simple but profitable. Only a gold pan was required. The more ambitious might build a sluice box, long tom, or cradle to obtain gold flakes from the gravel in the streams running off Baldy. With the discovery of a rich lode near the headwaters of Ute Creek, it would be necessary to bring more complicated and expensive machinery into the area. But the profits would make such expenditures worthwhile.

Although overshadowed by readily profitable placer mining, some quartz exploration and development had been carried out during the earliest years of the Moreno district. While at first sidetracked by their placer discoveries, Kelley and his comrades later did development work on the Mystic Lode. Digging a 300-foot tunnel, they found considerable gold in addition to the expected copper ore. Apparently the size of the vein or the value of the gold was not as high as expected, for plans were soon abandoned.

The first step toward exploration of a very rich vein of ore was taken when Tom Foley and Matthew Lynch, Willow Creek prospectors, with Robert Dougherty sneaked past Maxwell and prospected Ute Creek on the eastern side of Baldy in May 1867. They found rich deposits of placer gold in the creek bed, but apparently gave up their work without any development or attempt to trace the gold to its source.

Hard rock miners hand drilling a rich vein of ore.
Library of Congress Prints and Photographs Division, Public Domain Images.

A year later the three returned, panning carefully upstream until they no longer found gold in the gravel. They then searched the slopes above that point for likely outcroppings that marked the source. On a spur running off Baldy Mountain they found a thirty-foot depression full of decomposing quartz that shimmered with gold. Further exploration showed three well-defined veins, each three feet wide and a foot apart.

Maxwell soon learned of the discovery and, together with Lynch, V.S. Shelby of Santa Fe, John Dold, and Colonel E.R. Bergmann, they filed location papers on the claim. They called the mine the Aztec.

Before long mining men throughout the West knew of the Aztec discovery. Morris Bloomfield, a local storekeeper, saw a chunk of the ore and exclaimed: "If all is like it, one or two tons of this rock would be a fortune for anyone." Editor John T. Russell of the *Santa Fe Weekly Gazette* was more conservative when he declared that Bloomfield's story of ore assaying $10,000 per ton were just too fantastic to be believed. Shortly he swallowed his skeptical tongue because when Maxwell sent a sample of the ore to the US Assay Office in Denver, the results showed that each ton of Aztec ore would be worth over $19,000. The word spread rapidly.

One editor took three weeks to work over his figures and computed Lucien Maxwell's wealth. Assuming the presence of only one hundred tons of ore, Maxwell and his partners would make two million dollars, "a princely sum indeed," from the mine. If perchance it turned out to be very large, the baron of Cimarron would shortly "be known as the richest gold producer in the world."

Maxwell began at once to develop the mine. He sent an engineer to Chicago to buy a 15-stamp mill, each 435-pound stamp would crush ore against an iron base thirty-three times a minute, breaking the ore into find powder for further processing. With a twelve horsepower steam engine, the entire apparatus cost $8,000. Before the equipment arrived, Maxwell's men had constructed a frame building from local pine timber cut at his new sawmill on Ute Creek. Installed in the new building, the machinery went through its initial testing and started work on October 29, 1868.

The whole milling operation, under superintendent Edward H. Bergmann, required only five men, and Maxwell marveled at its success. In the first six days of operation the machinery extracted 120 ounces of gold valued at over $2,500. Mining men estimated that the Aztec would bring in a yearly profit of $109,500 if run at the same rate for only three hundred days a year. Surely Maxwell had found his bonanza at last.

Section of a stamp
mill showing five
stamps for crushing
gold ore.

Library of Congress
Prints and Photographs
Division, Public Domain
Images.

Stimulated by such success, other hard rock mining soon began. A man called "Big Jack" discovered a rich lode just south of the Aztec, and soon the Montezuma Mine was rivaling the nearby Aztec. Professor T.G. Rounds opened a mine he called the Swansea, while a Frenchman named Henry Buruel began work on the French Henry. By early 1869 a whole community of miners was at work near Baldy Mountain, by now the most important mining district in New Mexico.

The Creation of Colfax County

As hundreds, then thousands, of miners swarmed into northern New Mexico in search of gold, they naturally assembled in new towns and communities. During the first summer William H. Moore, George Buck, and other pioneer miners asked T.G. Rowe to survey a town site, layout out blocks of lots in checkerboard fashion with wide streets between them. The local citizens paid tribute to Moore, who had been instrumental in organizing the early Fort Union interests, by naming the new town "Elizabethtown" after his daughter.

Before long a village was rising in the wilderness. By June there were five small mercantile businesses—together equal to "half a country store," one visitor remarked—selling supplies to the prospectors. a month later twenty buildings were completed and another twenty were under construction.

Activity in the lively camp diminished during the winter when freezing weather and water shortages ended sluicing operations. While some miners left for bigger towns to await the spring thaw, many remained in Elizabethtown. Especially popular were buildings like the May Flower Saloon where cold miners warmed "the inner as well as the outer man."

Once again in 1868 Elizabethtown was "on the boom." It was rough and wild, yet pretended to have a certain class. Successful placer and lode operations in the vicinity of the village had attracted many new prospectors, and some were accompanied by their wives and children. In place of temporary shacks and tents which cluttered the town site during the first frantic summer, well-constructed homes and stores soon faced the streets of Elizabethtown. Slowly the town took on the air of permanence and respectability.

The progressiveness of the area was reflected in increasing demands for the creation of a separate government district. After two years of urging, the New Mexico Territorial Legislature heeded the call and established a new county on January 25, 1869, naming it after then US Vice President-elect Schuyler Colfax, who was visiting the West at that time.

Although his fame has since dwindled, Colfax was one of the most prominent politicians of his day. Born in New York City in 1823, he had moved to Indiana and worked his way up in the politics of that state. He was elected to the US Congress as a Re-

Elizabethtown as seen around 1870, view looking east toward Baldy.
Elizabethtown Museum Collection, Elizabethtown, New Mexico.

publican in 1855, serving as Speaker of the House for almost a decade before his nomination as Grant's Vice President in 1868. Like some of his contemporaries, Colfax was implicated in taking bribes and selling his influence, although he escaped censure or conviction on any of the charges.

Few towns could rival Elizabethtown in its claim to be Colfax County's seat of government. Early in March the residents of the area went to the polls to select their first officials. Maxwell was elected as probate judge, receiving virtually unanimous support from the citizens of Cimarron and Ute Creek, both of which he owned. H.J. Calhoun was elected sheriff, and the voters decided to retain Elizabethtown as the county seat.

But even more honors awaited the little town. On February 3, 1870, the mining village was incorporated by the territorial legislature, which was the first New Mexican town to be so honored. A convention of citizens met on March 18th and nominated candidates for mayor and councilmen. Early the next month, H.S. Russell, Colfax County's first legislator and the man mainly responsible for getting the town incorporated, was elected mayor over John E. Wheelock, a "popular and worthy gentleman."

Even as the county seat, Elizabethtown had difficulty supporting a newspaper. The first weekly in the valley, the *Moreno Lantern*, appeared in the summer of 1869, but was short-lived. It was followed by the *Elizabethtown Telegraph* and *Elizabethtown Argus*, neither of which seemed able to make a go of it.

By far the most interesting paper, however, was *The Thunderbolt*, which printed only three issues. When it appeared on the streets of Elizabethtown on February 20, 1871, miners throughout the district scurried to obtain copies. Priced at an outrageous 25¢ the four-page publication was sponsored by an anonymous association which pledged "to revive again liberty of the press and free public opinion in this country." The happy-go-lucky miners responsible for its printing pledged to change the editorship weekly because "too long an occupation in that exalted position would be considered detrimental to the Editorial peepers." They printed serious and comical attacks on well-known figures as well as popular miners in the area. Any county seat that could bring forth such a publication had certainly come of age.

Life at Maxwell's Ranch

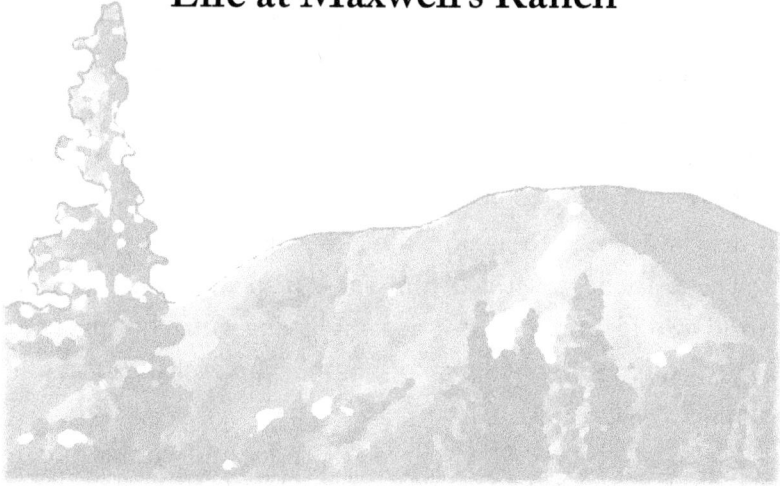

The New Wealth of Lucien Maxwell

No one profited more from the discovery of gold on Baldy than Lucien Maxwell. In addition to profitable contracts for feeding the local Indians and sales of cattle, sheep, and grain to settlers, Maxwell now took in additional money from his Aztec and Montezuma mines. Leases of placer claims to eager miners coupled with sales of supplies to gold-seekers added considerably to his income. By 1868 Maxwell's annual income amounted to nearly $50,000, and he had become one of the wealthiest men in New Mexico.

As the name of Lucien Maxwell spread throughout the Southwest and even to distant eastern cities, stories of his eccentricities also spread far and wide. One visitor reported that despite the large quantities of cash which Maxwell frequently had at his Cimarron mansion, he steadfastly refused to obtain a safe. Instead, he kept his money, frequently amounting to $30,000 in gold, silver, greenbacks, and government drafts, in the bottom drawer of an old bureau, "the most antiquated concern of common pine imaginable."

When a friend suggested that Maxwell would be wise to purchase a more secure vault, the Cimarron landowner only smiled, and while "a strange resolute look flashed from his dark eye," answered, "God help the man who attempted to rob me and I knew him."

Maxwell's reply typified the unbending, autocratic character which he seemed to assume after the discovery of gold on his ranch. A friend described him as "a man that nothing in the world would prevent from accomplishing what he undertook to do," adding that he knew of no one who ever dared stand in Maxwell's way.

To most visitors Maxwell was friendly and cordial. To the employees who dealt with him on an everyday basis he was an absolute tyrant, acting "just as if he owned the whole outfit." Calvin Jones, who worked for Maxwell in the 1860s described his employer's treatment of those who displeased him:

> If a Mexican servant didn't suit him or did anything against his order, he took a board or plank or anything he could get hold of and whipped him with it. I knew him to tie up one man and shave off the side of his head close to the skin with a butcher knife, then he struck him fifteen or twenty lashes with a cowhide and told him if he ever caught him on the place again he would kill him. Some twelve or fifteen years later he came back with a bunch of stolen horses and Maxwell did kill him.

On a much more favorable side, Maxwell must be praised for the hospitality which he showed to everyone visiting his Cimarron home. Miners on their way to Elizabethtown or Baldy, military officers coming or going from New Mexico assignments, stagecoach passengers whose trip had been delayed by high water

Maxwell mansion as it appeared in the 1870s.
Arthur Johnson Memorial Library Collection, Raton, New Mexico.

or broken equipment were all welcome to stay at Maxwell's for as long as they wished—providing, that is, that they did not somehow earn the displeasure of their host.

Maxwell did not expect payment for such services. In fact, any offer to pay was taken as an insult. One morning as the stage passengers prepared to resume their journey after a night at Cimarron, a well-dressed New Yorker asked the driver to point out the landlord to him. Directed to Maxwell, the man asked him how much breakfast cost. When the wealthy landowner replied that he expected nothing, the easterner insisted that he did not want favors and would pay for what he had. Maxwell became irritated and answered gruffly, "Well, then, it is $20." The easterner looked at Maxwell in astonishment for a moment before handing him a crisp twenty-dollar bill. Without saying a word, the lord of Cimarron stepped to a nearby fireplace and threw the greenback into the flames.

Maxwell's eccentricity also manifested itself in gambling. Nearly every night he played seven-up poker or some other popular card game with anyone staying at the house. If he won, Maxwell always demanded payment of every last cent. But often the next morning he would give or loan his losing opponent five hundred or a thousand dollars to tide them over.

Even more than card playing, Maxwell enjoyed horse racing. Before the discovery of gold he employed Squire T. Hart especially to train and care for his horses. For the next six years Hart lived at Cimarron, training horses in preparation for the prospect of a race. At least once a week and sometimes more often, Maxwell's fleet animals were matched against the finest in New Mexico. Hart remembered that Maxwell lost more often than he won, but others insisted that this was only because of unscrupulous jockeys who defrauded him of immense sums.

Worsening Indian Problems

While Lucien Maxwell was becoming almost legendary, other people in the Cimarron area were suffering under the changed conditions brought on by the discovery of precious metals on the land grant. The hardest hit were the very people who had generated the discovery, the Utes and Jicarillas living at Maxwell's ranch.

In addition to the inept and disinterested management which had long plagued their agency, the increasing population in the area caused new problems. Military men and then church representatives would take over the administration in the years that followed, but each agent was as unsuccessful as his predecessor. Friction between settlers and Indians became increasingly common until a full-scale war seemed unavoidable. Attempts to remove the natives from fast-growing Cimarron were constantly frustrated so that conditions remained critical throughout the 1870s.

The Indians foresaw trouble as soon as swarms of Anglo miners began arriving in the Baldy area in the spring of 1867. The mountains of that district had long been their home—a place where they might retreat from their plains enemies, where they had been born, and where their ancestors were buried. Now the Utes and Jicarillas became increasingly uneasy as they saw the area filling with mineral seekers.

The Utes were also dissatisfied because of a treaty which their chief, Keneatche, and other representatives of the tribe had signed in 1868 agreeing to move them to a new wilderness reservation in the San Juan country of southern Colorado. When the headmen returned to Cimarron after signing the document, the men of the tribe repudiated their actions, dismissed Keneatche and the others, and refused to obey the treaty. In this manner they expected the government to nullify the agreement. Instead their agent now reported that the annual allotments of blankets, agricultural tools, and food could be obtained only at the new agency in Colorado. Still the Indians steadfastly refused to leave Cimarron.

In Washington, DC, many lawmakers now realized that a major reorganization was necessary to end the inefficient and corrupt practices in the Indian Bureau. The national heroes of the day were soldiers who had just beaten the Confederates and saved the Union, so it was natural that Congress voted to place military officers at the head of each agency.

Mounted Indian warriors holding a council of war.
Library of Congress Prints and Photographs Division, Public Domain Images.

At Cimarron such a change was especially timely, since the government was continuing its efforts to move the natives to Colorado. Many felt that only military men would be able to persuade the Indians to go peacefully. The man selected to take charge of the agency was Captain Alexander S.B. Keyes, a career soldier from Massachusetts, who assumed command on August 17, 1869.

Soon after Keyes reached Cimarron, he realized the enormous task ahead of him. Neglected by their agent during the height of the gold rush, the natives were now without clothing and blankets necessary for the coming winter. Unless they were supplied, he was certain that it would be impossible even to consider moving them to Colorado.

The required goods did not come, however, and when the 1,500 Indians appeared for their annual allotments late in October, Keyes has only 39 blankets on hand. He gave what provisions he could to the natives, sending them off on a hunt with promises that the blankets would be there when they returned in mid-December. Then he fired off an angry letter to Santa Fe pleading for the blankets and suggesting that the useless items being sent, such as tableware and beaver traps, might be replaced with something useful.

When the needed items were not forthcoming, Lucien Maxwell, who had lived among the Utes and Jicarillas for nearly twenty-five years, sensed impending trouble. He pleaded with commanding general William N. Grier—the same man who had previously commanded troops at Rayado—for assistance. "There is an imminent danger of a general uprising against the settlements," Maxwell warned, and "unless prompt measures be taken to anticipate and prevent the outbreak, it will be sure and terrible."

For once such appeals fell on responsive ears, and soon a cavalry force of 100 men arrived at Maxwell's ranch. The officer in charge was instructed to avoid a conflict with the restless natives, but if they commenced any hostilities he should "attack and pursue them and not return until he has driven them west of the mountains." The arrival of the troopers at Cimarron in mid-December and the acquisition of 450 more blankets quieted the Indians at least temporarily and prevented continued depredations on the livestock of local residents.

The Dilemma of Captain Keyes

Once the Indians had been quieted by the presence of soldiers and the arrival of winter supplies, Captain Keyes had time to deal with several other problems that confronted him. Hoping to avoid the costs to Maxwell for providing supplies to the Indian agency and soldiers, a determined campaign was now being waged in Colorado to force the Indians to be moved to that state. When a "reliable officer of the army" exposed the "real" situation at Cimarron, the *Colorado Tribune* jumped at the opportunity to publicize his report of a visit to Maxwell's early in January 1870.

> The rumors of war were started by Maxwell and he succeeded in getting a troop of cavalry stationed on his ground, for nothing in God's name but to sell them grain and forage. I also saw Capt. Keyes, who claims to be agent for what are known as Maxwell's Utes and a few bands of Apaches. He has goods and makes issues to them. He is young and sweet on Maxwell's daughter. The milk in the cocoanut is satisfactorily accounted for."

Captain Keyes would not take such a personal attack quietly and quickly wrote the paper to demand the name of the letter writer so that he might challenge him to a duel at the first opportunity. He also sent his mother in Massachusetts an account of the incident to forward to Senator Henry Wilson of his home state. He had been "shoved around enough" and now petitioned the Senator to return him to the regular Army where he would no longer be "lied about and left to the mercy of such kind of men as grow here." As for the Ute and Jicarilla agency, Keyes suggested that the government might do better to send a Quaker than a military officer to handle the Indians.

In spite of his denials, the reports published in Colorado may not have been as untrue as Captain Keyes would have his mother and the senator believe. At least his romance with Virginia Maxwell proved to be true. The young daughter of Cimarron's monarch had been raised according to the Spanish tradition of feminine isolation before being sent to a St. Louis convent for formal education. Returning to Cimarron, she soon met and fell in love with the handsome young Protestant Indian agent. After a short courtship they decided to marry.

Virginia approached Reverend Thomas Harwood, a Methodist circuit rider who periodically visited Cimarron, asking him to perform the ceremony. At last Harwood agreed, even though he knew that her powerful father would never approve of the match. When he arrived in Cimarron on March 30, 1870, Virginia had all the arrangements made. Harwood himself later recalled the occasion:

> No army general could have planned for a battle more wisely than she had planned for this marriage. She had made a confidant of Mrs. Rinehardt, a Methodist and the miller's wife. It was Indian ration day. There would be hundreds of Apaches at the mill to draw rations of meat and flour. 'Mr. Keyes is their agent,' said Miss Maxwell, 'and will be there to issue rations to the Indians. Mrs. Rinehardt and I will go down to the mill at 4 pm ... You must go down a little before that and go up into the third story of the mill.'"

Everything went exactly as planned. When the clergyman reached the third level of Maxwell's stone mill, he found the room swept and carpeted with various kinds of robes in anticipation of the ceremony to be performed there. When the young

Virginia Maxwell Keyes with two of her granddaughters.
Her marriage was a happy and lasting one.
Arthur Johnson Memorial Library Collection, Raton, New Mexico.

couple appeared, Harwood held the marriage, only Rinehardt and his wife being present as witnesses.

Keyes and his bride dared not reveal their secret, however, for fear of Maxwell's action on hearing that his daughter had married without even consulting him. Throughout April the couple anxiously awaited word of the captain's requested transfer. Official orders relieving him of the post and stationing him at Fort Sill, Indian Territory, were issued April 2nd, but even then delays in the arrival of his successor kept Keyes in New Mexico until early May. When Keyes and his wife were safely on the stage bound eastward, the bridegroom handed the driver a copy of their marriage certificate to be delivered to Lucien Maxwell at Cimarron.

The Maxwell Land Grant Company

Land Grant for Sale

Although Maxwell was probably angry at hearing that his daughter had run off with the good-looking eastern soldier, his anger may have been lessened by other happier events transpiring at the same time. Throughout 1869 negotiations had been underway which would eventually result in the sale of the massive Maxwell property, while further upsetting the Utes and Apaches who roamed the mountains near Cimarron.

Early in the year Jerome B. Chaffee, George M. Chilcott, and Charles F. Holly, all successful Colorado mining men, approached Maxwell about the purchase of his interest in the property. No doubt Maxwell realized that the growing population of the region required more careful and expert management than he was capable or desirous of giving it. Moreover, questions as to the validity of his title to the land were already being raised which would surely grow as its value increased.

If Maxwell could negotiate a cash sale while interest was high, turn over future development of the grant to others, and retire with his profits, he would be certain of life-long financial security without managerial responsibilities. He could devote his time to card playing, horse racing, and other more enjoyable activities. Therefore, on May 26, 1869, Maxwell gave the Colorado trio an option to buy the grant, excluding for himself the 1,000-acre home ranch and buildings on it.

Maxwell immediately employed attorney John S. Watts of Santa Fe, with whom he was simultaneously attempting to develop the fledgling town of Virginia City in the Moreno Valley. Watts began to negotiate with the Surveyor General of New Mexico to have the ranch surveyed. Maxwell deposited $5,500 to pay for the survey and on June 5th Surveyor General T. Rush Spencer contracted with William W. Griffin, an influential Santa Fe Republican, to do the work.

However, when the contract was submitted to the General Land Office in Washington, DC, for approval, it was speedily rejected on the suspicion that the proposed survey would include more than the maximum of eleven square leagues of land which Mexican governors had the power to grant to any one man. Thus began a dispute over the proper and legal boundaries of the land grant which would last for over a quarter century.

As soon as he heard of the rejection, Maxwell conferred with the prospective purchasers and their attorneys who prepared a lengthy legal reply supporting Maxwell's claim of title to the land. On June 21, 1860 the US Congress had confirmed the grant, on the recommendation of the Surveyor General, with the sole qualification that they were relinquishing only the rights of the United States and in no way jeopardizing the claim of any other person. No opposing claim had ever been raised, and Maxwell insisted that the title had been valid when he bought the grant. Never had he suspected that the government, "which

had pledged its faith to that of Mexico and had by solemn legisla-
tive act 'quit claimed and
relinquished' all its right,"
should after a quarter of
a century call into ques-
tion his ownership.

Subsequently argued
and reargued in courts
from one side of the con-
tinent to the other, from
the level of Justice of the Peace
to the Supreme Court of the United
States, and by some of the nation's most competent lawyers, this
was the basic argument for the confirmation of the grant which
was eventually upheld. But before the final US Supreme Court
decision came, thousands of pages would be filled by both sides,
thousands of dollars would be spent in legal fees, and many lives
would be lost in the accompanying fight.

Upon receipt of Maxwell's appeal and other evidence of the
extent and validity of the grant, Secretary of the Interior Jacob
D. Cox ruled on the request, and at the same time set down a
guideline which he hoped would be used on other similar cases. The boundaries of the Beaubien-Miranda grant were given
according to natural features of the topography, he noted, and
gave no clue as to the extent of the land claimed. The only evidence Congress could rely upon when it was making the 1860
confirmation was Beaubien's personal statement that he claimed
only fifteen to eighteen leagues. Now, however, it appeared that
Maxwell was claiming upwards of 450 square leagues or almost
2,000,000 acres. To settle this and all similar matters Cox declared:

It is therefore my opinion and you may receive it as the rule for this and all like cases that where a Mexican colonization grant is confirmed without measurement of boundaries or of distinct specification of the quantity confirmed, in statute or in the report upon which confirmation was made, no greater quantity than eleven leagues to each claimant shall be surveyed and set off to them, that such quantity shall be surveyed in tracts of eleven square leagues each, the general position of such tracts to be selected by the grantee and the tract to be then surveyed as compactly as practicable.

Thus the government had laid down its basic argument: No matter what Maxwell might claim, the original tract could not include more than a total of 22 square leagues allotted for the two original claimants.

Searching for Investors in the Land Grant

Seeming to ignore the adverse decision of the Secretary of the Interior, Chilcott, Chaffee, and Holly were meanwhile busily seeking purchasers for the grant. Chaffee prepared and had printed an elaborate report which described all aspects of the estate in glowing terms and assured prospective buyers that the title to it was "complete and perfect."

As described in the first promotional booklet, the grant was truly a paradise on earth. "It is accessible, it has hospitable climate, it is in the immediate vicinity of large agricultural resources, immense beds of coal, and surrounded with never-ending quantities of timber." After several weeks of personal investigation in the region, Chaffee assured his readers that he was more certain than ever of the tremendous potential of the area. With the steady development of the "Great West," the value of this grant would certainly increase immeasurably.

The sales campaign thus instigated by the Colorado men paid quick dividends as Europeans began showing interest in the vast

New Mexico tract. Particularly interested was a group of London investors led by John Collinson. Maxwell and the Coloradoans crossed the continent to New York to complete final arrangements for transferring the estate. January 28, 1870, the Colorado trio negotiated a new option to buy the property from Maxwell within six months for $1,350,000.

The same day they assigned their option to the newly organized Maxwell Land Grant and Railway Company which bought the grant for the agreed price on April 30, 1870, with the exception of the home ranch, Maxwell's interest in the Aztec and Montezuma Mines, and other business property retained by Maxwell or previously transferred to others.

Maxwell Land Grant Company promotional booklet.

Public Domain Image from Archive.org.

Because the laws of New Mexico did not authorize foreigners to hold real estate, a local board of directors was quickly organized by the promoters. Its members, consisting of territorial governor William A. Pile, ex-Surveyor General T. Rush Spencer, and attorney John S. Watts, retained nominal control of the ranch through the Maxwell Land Grant and Railway Company which they incorporated on May 12, 1870.

Meanwhile the new owners had published another much more elaborate brochure to attract financial support in Europe. Authored by Collinson, who effectively took control of the company, and William A. Bell, a London doctor who had visited the grant with an early railroad survey party, several editions and thousands of copies of the booklet were issued. Besides the earlier statements that the title was unquestioned, the promoters now included certificates from the leading attorneys in both the United States and England that the land grant was genuine. The certificates were issued by John Watts, who could now advertise himself as Chief Justice of New Mexico Territory, William M. Everts, the ex-United States Attorney General who had gained fame by successfully defending President Andrew Johnson during impeachment proceedings, and Judah P. Benjamin, the Confederate cabinet member who fled to England following the Civil War.

More interesting still were the elaborate descriptions of the financial status of the grant. John Howell, who had managed Maxwell's agricultural enterprises for some years, certified that in producing almost 100,000 bushels of grain during the previous year plus considerable corn, oats, and hay, the Cimarron landowner would earn nearly $100,000. From high on Aztec Ridge, mine manager E.H. Bergmann was even more optimistic. Gross income from the Aztec had amounted to almost $50,000, while placer and hydraulic mining had brought in about the same amount. In all, the promotional booklet advertised Maxwell's income for a single year would exceed $250,000.

But, the promoters claimed, Maxwell had done little to capitalize on the potential of his New Mexico property. The arrival of railroads would increase the land value exponentially. Within a few years thousands of farmers would be eager to buy the rich lands. Gold miners would continue flocking to work productive streams and locate rich lodes. For anyone wishing to find an ideal investment, the Maxwell Land Grant was picture perfect.

Although many of the statements included in this and numerous later brochures were certainly exaggerated and often blatant falsehoods, thousands of Europeans who believed them bought stock in the new company. Others subscribed to bond issues which the grant promoters made. Not until years later would they all learn of the problems involved with developing the property.

Lucien Maxwell in Retirement

As word spread through New Mexico that the vast land grant had been sold and its owner was going into retirement, his friends wished him success. The editor of the Santa Fe *New Mexican* wrote: "We congratulate Mr. Maxwell on so advantageous a sale, and the company on the acquisition of a property which, under their jurisdiction and skillful management, will unquestionably yield a handsome return."

Maxwell had no sooner returned from New York than he began to make plans to invest the money he had received. On September 3, 1870, he met at Cimarron with Virginia City promoters Henry N. Hooper and Charles F. Holly, Judge Watts, and Maxwell's son Peter, to organize the First National Bank of Santa Fe.

Maxwell provided the entire capital of $150,000, retaining 1270 shares of stock. He gave 200 shares to Holly and ten each to his son, Watts, and Hooper, who would constitute the ruling

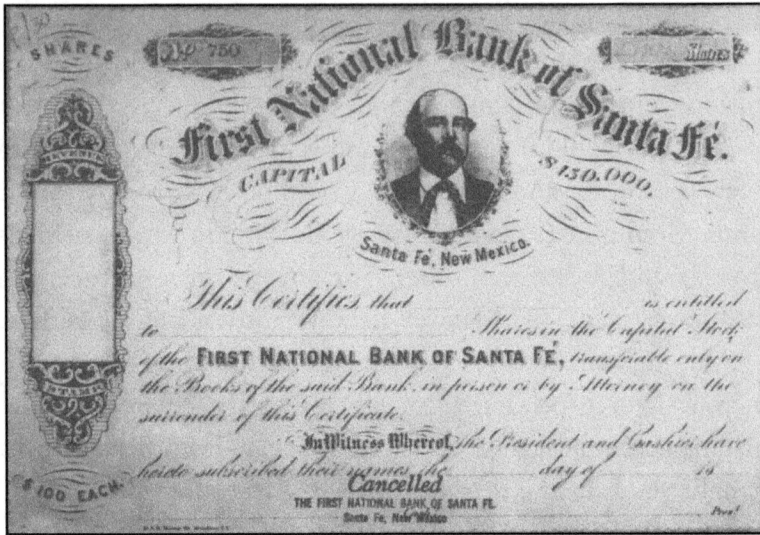

First National Bank of Santa Fe stock certificate,
featuring a portrait of Lucien Maxwell.

Arthur Johnson Memorial Library Collection, Raton, New Mexico.

board of the bank. At their organizational meeting the men also approved an official seal for the bank—a wild Indian surrounded by "The First National Bank of Santa Fe"—which has been retained to the present day. On motion of Judge Watts they also ordered 3,000 certificates of stock bearing Maxwell's portrait to be printed.

Maxwell then addressed a letter to Comptroller of Currency, N.R. Hulburt, applying to have his institution named a national bank. It would be the only such bank in New Mexico or within 400 miles of Santa Fe, he wrote, declaring his intention to manage it "in conformity with the law and your instructions." On December 13, 1870, the bank was issued National Bank charter No. 1750 and soon thereafter Maxwell sent his cashier Charles Holly to New York to procure $135,000 in currency with which to commence business.

April 15, 1871, the First National Bank of Santa Fe opened it doors on the west side of the historic Santa Fe Plaza. Soon,

Officers' Quarters at Fort Sumner, New Mexico, where
Lucien & Luz Maxwell retired after leaving Cimarron.

Arthur Johnson Memorial Library Collection, Raton, New Mexico.

however, a rival National Bank of New Mexico opened, putting
the squeeze on Maxwell's operation. Less than a month after the
opening of his bank, Maxwell sold out his interest to a group of
Santa Fe politicians led by lawyers Stephen B. Elkins and Thomas B. Catron. Under their operation and subsequent owners the
institution has continued in operation to the present day, still
one of the most important financial institutions in the state.

Even more disheartening financially was Maxwell's investment in the railroad business. According to stories, he put nearly
a quarter of a million dollars into a construction company which
was organized to build the Texas Pacific Railroad through the
southwest. When it failed, he lost his entire investment.

After the arrival of Collinson's representatives in Cimarron,
Maxwell left his old home, having meanwhile sold his remaining
interest in the town and his Baldy mines to the Englishmen. He
took up residence at the abandoned Fort Sumner Indian Reservation along the Pecos River in southeastern New Mexico. There
he lived quietly until his death five years later on July 25, 1875.

The Englishmen in Control

Having purchased what they considered the richest piece of property in North America, John Collinson and his British associates soon began arriving in Cimarron, prepared to reap fortunes from their investment. Initially their glowing talk was backed up with considerable action. To promote its activities and spread word of the grant's glory, the company established the *Cimarron News*, "devoted particularly to advancing the Maxwell Land Grant."

Before long these activities had spread to Elizabethtown, where editor Will Dawson met with local opposition after taking up the Britisher's line. When pressure from the miners grew too great, Dawson merged his paper with the one in Cimarron to create the *News and Press*. It became the official voice of the foreigners, with editors that included Frank Springer and William Koogler.

Equally spectacular programs were being carried out along political lines, and the promoters soon had the Colfax County seat moved to Cimarron where their business activities would be centered. Before long company favorites controlled all the political offices. Maxwell's house was repainted and filled with expensive imported furnishings. Serving as the company headquarters, it assumed the elegance and beauty too often lacking during Maxwell's time. Today many a Colfax County collector boasts of Maxwell house furniture, which testifies to the good taste of Collinson and his successor, Frank R. Sherwin. In addition, the Englishmen drew up the first official plat map of the village of Cimarron, with lot boundaries and regularly spaced roads replacing the previous haphazard arrangements. Many streets bore the names of land grant officials, with Collinson Avenue becoming an important thoroughfare.

Not long after their arrival, however, the Englishmen realized that securing profits from the grant would not be as easy as they at first expected. The rich Aztec Mine, which had constantly poured cash into Maxwell's coffers, closed down because of poor management and declining ore values. Attempts to reopen it were expensive and yielded few returns. Moreover, continuing Indian problems discouraged many easterners from settling on the grant. Once the Utes and Jicarillas were finally removed in 1876, a major source of income dried up. Without the Indian agents and Army officers to purchase grain and meat, prices declined and profits dropped.

Probably the major reason for the company's trouble resulted from the fact that they could not wield the authority that Lucien Maxwell had. No one had dared question the previous landowner's authority—miners grudgingly paid him rent for their leases, settlers accepted his terms, and laborers worked for exceptionally low wages. But once the accented foreigners arrived with their newfangled ideas and peculiar methods, the situation changed and opposition grew rapidly.

As if to magnify these local problems, a national economic depression hit in 1873. Brought on by over-investment and excessive speculation—of which the land grant was a good example—the panic opened with the failure of Jay Cooke and Company, well-known Philadelphia investment brokers. Before long companies everywhere were declaring bankruptcy, closing their doors, and putting workers on the street. By the summer of 1875 they were joined by the Maxwell Land Grant and Railway Company, which was unable to pay its employees' salaries or its local taxes.

Social Unrest and Legal Disputes

The Colfax County War

Far more colorful and dramatic than the English company's financial troubles was an open declaration of war against the foreign owners of the Maxwell Grant by local settlers. The tragic aspects of this quarrel have been repeated in historical and even fictional works many times. In fact, only the Lincoln County War and Billy the Kid attract greater interest in all of New Mexico's modern history. Instead of recalling the dispute in detail, however, it will be our purpose here to analyze the causes and the results of the decade of fighting. Some of the lesser known historical aspects will also be described.

In many ways the Colfax County War can be compared to the American Revolution. Our colonial forefathers arrived along the eastern coast of North America in the 1600s, only to learn that they were essentially on their own, taking up land, building houses, creating governments with very little attention from the authorities in Britain. But after 1763 the English attempted to reassert their power by taxing and controlling the settlers, provoking a revolution. The revolt soon assumed additional social significance. The poor and oppressed viewed it as a way to better themselves, overthrowing the entrenched local leadership, and expelling the hated landlords once and for all.

Similar events transpired in northern New Mexico. More interested in his card playing and horse racing than in efficiently managing his estate, Lucien Maxwell had neglected the grant. Farmers, miners, and timbermen moved into Colfax County and began to exercise control over the property they occupied. Few even considered that the Cimarron man owned the whole vast region as his own property.

When legal questions arose about the grant's validity, the settlers became increasingly uncooperative. Then the British arrived, ordering anyone occupying land to purchase their property, arrange lease agreements, or move out. Similar to the circumstances that provoked the American revolution, social antipathy increased. Because they were frequently associated with the company, the wealthy, the political and social elite, drew first fire. By expelling them from power and office, many settlers began to dream of a new order where they would be in control of their own destiny.

Naturally, opposition originated among the miners, not only the most numerous but also the most vocal and least easily intimidated of the county's residents. When they learned of the property transfer, the men called a meeting on September 3, 1870, to "duly and dispassionately" decide what action should be taken. Insisting that their rights to the mineral grounds were superior to either those of the company or the Indians, they agreed to negotiate leases only if the Britishers could show a valid United States government patent which specifically delineated the grant's boundaries.

Peaceful meetings rapidly gave way to violence. On the night of October 23, 1870, a riot broke out in Elizabethtown brought on by the election of R.H. Longwill, a company supporter, as probate judge. Edmund Luff, commanding L Troop, 8th Cavalry, which was stationed in the area, refused to stop the riots until requested to do so by the civil authorities. After the home of Justice of the Peace John McBride was burned, the company's supporters pleaded to Santa Fe for help. Lt. Cobb immediately led twenty-one men to the Moreno Valley to stop the violence, while acting governor Henry Wetter "authorized and ordered" civil officers to take measures to protect "the lives and property of citizens."

Even though that disturbance was soon put down, even more serious trouble broke out the following spring. When a band of company officials marched up Ute Creek to collect rent, organized miners met them. "Unlawfully and violently combined together," the gold seekers disarmed the officials, held them as hostages, and captured considerable company property.

Harper's Weekly woodcut of angry mobs taking to the streets, setting fire to buildings and spreading violence.

Library of Congress Prints and Photographs Division, Public Domain Images.

This time Governor William A. Pile hurried north from the capital and ordered the miners to dissolve their organization and to abstain from violence. Anyone who was dissatisfied, he insisted, should submit his claims to the courts. To support this position, Pile saw to it that Major D.H. Clendenin and a force of soldiers raced from Fort Union to Cimarron. Again the troops succeeded, but now the miners began to leave the area in droves, further depressing the economy.

But even more serious revolts were soon spreading throughout the county. Not only miners but farmers, ranchers, and storekeepers were opposing the foreign company.

A Martyr for the Cause

Every revolution needs a martyr, someone who symbolizes the movement and sums up the feelings of its supporters. During the American Revolution, the Boston Massacre provided heroes aplenty. John Brown became an anti-slavery martyr during the Civil War. The children of Belgium, the fallen in the USS Arizona, and others have served more recently to rally supporters to a cause.

Methodist minister
Franklin J. Tolby.

Quentin Robinson Collection.

Colfax County's martyred hero was the Reverend F.J. Tolby, an itinerant Methodist preacher who served the area for several years. What previous role he had played in the growing land grant controversy is debatable. Some authorities insist that he had actively opposed the foreigners, while other evidence suggests that he was neutral or at least relatively inactive.

It was in death, however, that his importance grew. Having left Cimarron for a church service at Elizabethtown, the preacher never reached his destination. Several days later searchers found Tolby's body in Cimarron Canyon near a creek now bearing his name. Robbery was obviously not the motive, for his personal belongings had been left intact.

Why had the popular man of God been killed? Sufficient evidence was never collected to prove exactly who the murderer was, but people shared their own speculations. Some said it was probably a roving band of killers, while others said that a personal enemy had taken the minister's life. But the anti-grant forces blamed it all on the company or their henchmen, saying that Tolby had died for their cause.

Emotionalism increased rapidly after a "trial" which was soon held for a suspected killer. Certain that a Cimarron law officer named Cruz Vega knew something about the murder, or maybe even took part in it, a gang of settlers led by Reverend O.P. Mc-Mains decided to question him. William Low, a Moreno miner who also farmed on the Ponil, was induced to hire Vega to help him watch his cornfield one evening. As Low described it, the proceedings that night came as close to vigilante terrorism as anything in the area's history. Long after dark, Low and Vega were awakened by a band of five or six citizens who tossed a rope around Vega's neck and hauled him to a nearby telegraph pole.

Soon the rope had been looped across the line and stretched tight as the questioning began. McMains and his friends badgered the helpless man, lifting poor Vega off his feet every few seconds, then dropping him back down. His exact words were never recorded, but the mob was satisfied that he had committed the murder at the request of the land grant company. Even a confession did him little good, however, for the next morning Vega's body was found dangling from the telegraph pole. Marks on the body showed that torture had not been limited to the rope.

After Vega's death a full-scale war seemed about to break out in Colfax County. Threats were made against the lives of grant and anti-grant leaders alike. Local courts and law enforcement organizations were too packed with company supporters to receive any respect. Out of these disputes two new leaders arose who would assume prominence for the next decade. Reverend O.P. McMains became the settler's champion, while attorney Frank Springer took the lead for the new Dutch-controlled land grant company.

McMains versus Springer

As eastern newspapers screamed of civil war in Colfax County, local leaders feared for their lives. Both settlers and company officials issued charges and counter-charges until the controversy slowly moved from exchanging bullets to a war of words and lawsuits.

Unable to pay taxes or promote development of any sort, the Maxwell Land Grant Company finally was declared insolvent by the late 1870s. Following long, complicated, and frequently bitter negotiations, a new company headed by Dutch bondholders was created to take over the Britishers' assets and work out a new, more financially stable development program. Robbed by the speculation of Frank R. Sherwin, a notorious New York promoter who brought his talents to Cimarron for a time, the new organization verged on bankruptcy for several years, but by the 1880s it seemed at last to have achieved financial stability.

The man most responsible for this new vitality was attorney Frank Springer, certainly one of the ablest and most important men in Colfax County's history. An Iowa native who had been trained as both a scientist and a lawyer, he arrived in New Mexico in 1873 to edit the *Cimarron News and Press*.

As an officer and attorney for the land grant company, he saw the need to forego short-term profits in favor of long-term development. Issuing promotional brochures, writing newspaper articles, and generally promoting land grant interests, Springer soon became the company's most active officer. A legal expert of the highest order, he was also principally responsible for winning the Maxwell Land Grant Company's case before the US Supreme Court. In later years when he lived in Las Vegas, Santa Fe, and Philadelphia, he contributed to the cultural and artistic development of the Southwest, while winning world-wide fame for his studies in paleontology. At his death in 1927, New Mexicans mourned the loss of one of their most important leaders.

Rev. Oscar P. McMains.

Longmont Museum Collection.

Attorney Frank Springer.

Aztec Mill Museum Collection.

Springer found an able assistant in Harry Whigham, a Britisher who served the company as secretary and local manager for many years. A likeable young fellow who could work effectively with the settlers, Whigham did much to prevent further hostilities.

Throughout the 1880s, Springer was engaged in a bitter controversy with Reverend Oscar P. McMains, who represented the Colfax County settlers. After being acquitted of the murder of Cruz Vega—which he probably did not personally commit—the preacher proved untiring in his anti-grant efforts. He addressed countless meetings throughout the state, urging continued opposition to the Dutch company. At Raton he published a settlers' newspaper, *The Independent*, which became his mouthpiece. A constant barrage of letters, to everyone from President Grover Cleveland to the lowliest New Mexico settler, stirred up public opinion and aroused sympathy for the cause he represented.

Both Springer and McMains realized, however, that violence would not win them any victories. Continued fighting and killing would only inflame tempers while hindering the economic and social development of the area. If the Army were sent in or many people were killed, Colfax County might earn such a bad reputation that it could never again prosper. Slowly, therefore, the field of battle turned from the countryside to the courts, as briefs replaced bullets.

A Decision at Last

Long years passed before a final decision was handed down in the case of the *United States v. Maxwell Land Grant Company*. Originated in the local courts of New Mexico and Colorado, the matter was subsequently appealed to federal district court in Denver and finally to the United States Supreme Court.

Numerous problems arose during the course of litigation. Important documents had mysteriously disappeared from the territorial archives in Santa Fe. Opponents of the grant insisted that maps and papers had been altered in favor of the Dutchmen. Old residents testified that the earlier surveys had not been carried out as reported. Some even accused the company of perpetuating a tremendous fraud, not unlike the bogus claims of James Addison Reavis in Arizona.

The whole matter also involved the complicated issue of what Mexican law provided regarding the granting of land. Exactly how much land had Armijo intended to give Beaubien and Miranda? Had the governor's actions met the requirements of Mexican statutes? Were the papers and other documents indeed enough proof of the grant's legitimacy?

Not until the second week of March 1887 were formal hearings held before the nation's highest tribunal. William A. Maury, Assistant US Attorney General, was aided by Special Counsel J.A. Bently in presenting the government's and the settlers' case, while Frank Springer and Charles E. Gast represented the land grant company.

After considering all of the evidence, legal as well as historical, the court handed down its momentous decision on April 18, 1887. Even though the Beaubien-Miranda grant may not have included all the property that the Dutch claimed, Justice Miller wrote for the entire court, the Congressional act of confirmation on June 21, 1860, had conveyed all the property in dispute to the grantees. In short, the entire 1,714,764.93 acres of the land grant as claimed by the Dutch were their legal property. When a final appeal for rehearing was rejected, the settlers had lost their case. Disheartened and disillusioned, McMains moved to Colorado where he lived his remaining days in obscurity.

The decision marked the high point in Frank Springer's legal career. Praised by the court for his able presentation, the young Iowan had personally won a great victory. William A. Keleher, a noted attorney as well as historian, wrote:

Springer's zeal and learning, his outstanding ability as a lawyer, his great industry and persuasion, had never been put to a
greater test, or been more magnificently rewarded. Successful
termination of the litigation marked the zenith of his career as
a member of the bar in New Mexico.

More important than Springer's personal triumph, Colfax
County could now continue its development. Certain of retain-
ing possession of their property, cattlemen could improve their
ranches and introduce blooded stock. Farmers began talking of
irrigation projects, while new railroad facilities were added to
those already constructed. Even the Baldy mines witnessed a new
era of activity. Colfax County was one again on the rise.

Building Ranches and Farms

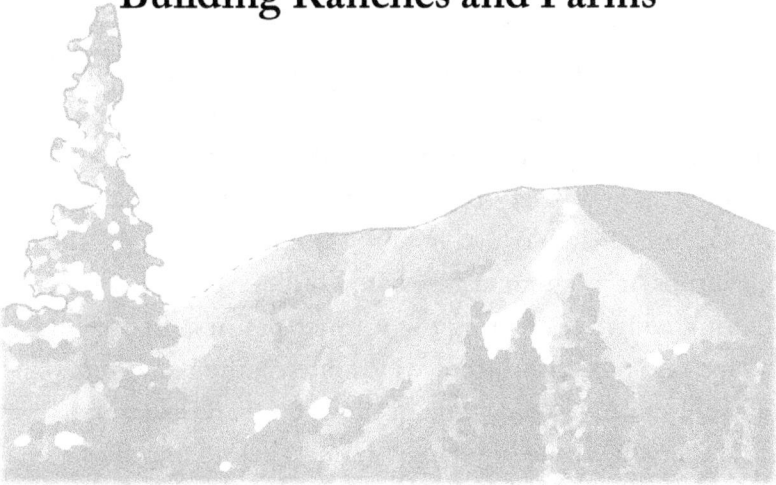

Cowboys and Cattlemen

Ranching had slowly developed during the 1870s, in spite of continued friction between settlers and grant owners. This occurred principally because of increased demand for beef. Locally, miners and townspeople were willing to pay premium prices. Nearby Denver provided an important market, while many stockmen drove their herds to railheads at Kit Carson, Colorado, and later Trinidad for transportation to eastern packing houses.

Early ranching was a hard, but often very profitable occupation. In the era of open ranges, few men owned large spreads, but by controlling water supplies and building a makeshift headquarters, they could control vast areas of unclaimed prairie. This was the heyday of the cowboy, who needed to keep a close and constant watch on his stock to be certain that they remained together and stayed healthy. Quality was far less important than quantity, and many animals were so scrawny that modern ranchers would probably laugh at them.

Weather conditions were the greatest worry. Since they had no supplementary feed available, the stockmen could lose an entire herd during a difficult winter or a long drought. Newspapers paid considerable attention to weather predictions, happily announcing rain and glorying over the lush grasses it would produce. But after a heavy snow, accounts of the number of dead animals and bankrupt owners filled the local columns.

Then as now, every cattleman tried to secure pasture which would furnish ample food in both summer and winter. The high mesa tops or mountain valleys proved ideal for summer grazing. During winter and spring the warmer prairies, especially those with some protection from wind, offered the best grass. When the rains failed to come or hard snows covered the ground, however, everyone rushed to sell his animals before they died of starvation.

In addition to the weather, wild animals constantly menaced Colfax County herds. The grizzly bears that had chased off early ranchers had been all but eliminated, but in the late nineteenth century roving packs of wolves became a tremendous problem. After a series of attacks, local citizens often gathered together for a wolf hunt, uniting to drive the animals into the open where they could be shot. Bounties for "wolf scalps" were high, reaching $15 each in 1899. Mountain lions and coyotes were less bothersome, although at times they became serious enough to disturb stockmen.

It was during this early period that many of Colfax County's most famous ranches were established. The Maxwell Cattle Company, a wholly-owned subsidiary of the grant company—the "Long H Outfit"—controlled the most land. Under the management of Francis Clutton, who later built his own ranch along Cimarroncito Creek near Cimarron, it became the most important producer in the area during the early 1880s. Two Brit-

Maxwell Cattle Company roundup crew, about 1892.
Aztec Mill Museum Collection, Cimarron, New Mexico.

ishers, Harold Wilson and Montague Stevens, along with their ranch manager William French, began the WS Ranch, which controlled 120,000 acres in Colfax County plus even more in southern New Mexico. A Denver man who made his first money in the Elizabethtown mining boom, H.M. Porter had an interest in several area ranches, along with Frank and Charles Springer, M.M. Chase, and others.

Once the Indians had been removed, the cattle business began to flourish in eastern Colfax County, which for many years extended all the way to the Texas Panhandle. With huge areas providing good pasture during at least part of the year, a permanent population soon began to inhabit the treeless plains. Sheep also became important in this area, although no examples of the famed sheepmen/cattlemen wars occurred in the area.

With so many cattle and so few lawmen, rustlers were less common than might have been expected. Although the legendary exploits of Clay Allison and Billy the Kid have be widely publicized and often grossly exaggerated, only occasionally did some desperado attempt to steal a few head of livestock. Like to-day's small-time robber, he was usually caught and imprisoned, although a few hangings did take place. Just as serious as rustling was brand changing. Many ranchers were aroused in 1880, for instance , then the county sheriff announced that Marion Hills-worth had been arrested for changing Long H brands into his own HHP marking.

The Irrigation Age

Water was the most important need of Colfax County ranch-ers and farmers. Without a sure supply to irrigate their alfalfa fields and water their livestock, agriculturalists might be com-pletely wiped out by a prolonged drought. But if water were available in sufficient amounts, truck farming, apple orchards, and the like might add to the areas' economic base.

Many irrigation projects were developed during the 1880s and 1890s. Most were relatively small in scope. Building a dam to capture creek water in a pond, a local rancher could then dig a system of ditches to carry the water to his nearby fields. Literally hundreds of small lakes resulting from the organized Springer Ditch System still dot the high plains from Raton to Springer.

The largest and most important irrigation project in the area was the vast Eagle Nest Dam to harness the Cimarron River for use by ranchers and farmers throughout the area. Conceived and financed under the direction of Frank Springer's brother Charles, its construction marked the high point in water development in northeastern New Mexico. Still invaluable to agriculturalists and an attraction to fishermen and water sports enthusiasts, the dam symbolized a new era for ranching.

The idea for damming the Cimarron River at the point where it left the Moreno Valley was not a new one. As early as 1888 surveyor Levi Preston estimated that a dam only 100 feet high would collect enough water to irrigate 54,000 acres of land.

Men and teams of horses dredge an irrigation ditch.
Library of Congress Prints and Photographs Division, Public Domain Images.

Aware of the practical need for dependable water supplies on his vast property, Charles Springer purchased the 600-acre dam site from the Maxwell Land Grant Company in 1906. Along with other land secured through legal agreements and purchases, Springer soon controlled enough land to build a 100,000 acre-foot reservoir.

Action began in mid-1907 when Charles Springer, A.H. Officer of the Maxwell Company, Frederick Whitney and George Remley of the Cimarron Townsite Company, incorporated the Cimarron Valley Land Company. Soon they announced a plan to build a huge reservoir at the junction of Moreno and Cieneguilla Creeks. A twenty-mile long irrigation ditch would carry the water through the mountains at a point between the Cimarron and Rayado Rivers.

Many businessmen and ranchers praised the project and volunteered to invest in the area after it had been completed. F. Wistzer of the American Beet Sugar Refining Company visited the region during the spring of 1908. Equally impressed with the fertile soil and relatively low cost of acquiring water, he predicted that Cimarron would soon be a great sugar producer, rivaling Rocky Ford, Colorado, or Garden City, Kansas.

Still construction did not get underway. Capitalists visited Cimarron with Springer again in 1911, but apparently they were not sufficiently impressed to provide the funds. That same year a group of ranchers including men from the Springer Ditch Company and French Tract Corporation joined Springer to organize another irrigation group. Their plans for building small dams and canals were soon put into action, but the larger canal project still did not begin.

Finally in 1916 Charles Springer, having grown impatient with the slow progress, vowed to "undertake the completion of the project for himself." By now he had also taken the time to purchase additional property which he planned to irrigate. When the experienced cattleman announced that he would provide water for 300,000 acres, the *Raton Reporter* echoed the view of many citizens: "No other project in the county...would ultimately do as much toward the future growth and prestige of the northern part of the state," it editorialized, calling for its completion with all due speed.

The Completion of Eagle Nest Dam

Before actual work could begin, two preparatory jobs had to be finished. Because the St. Louis, Rocky Mountain and Pacific Railway had a right-of-way to build their line into Moreno Valley, a railroad tunnel wide though for two locomotives had to be cut through the rock above the dam site. Secondly, the road from Ute Park to Elizabethtown and Taos had to be rerouted to bypass the dam site. By late 1916 and early 1917 there were 150 men at work on these projects.

Excitement grew as the massive dam project at last took shape. A temporary town near the dam housed hundreds of laborers recruited from around the state. Equipment and supplies poured in through Cimarron. Soon a massive 60-foot overhead trestle had been installed to lift cement into place. With the foundation work completed, the structure soon began to rise above water level.

Everywhere praise flowed for the efficient work of engineer Neal Hanson and his crews. Besides overcoming seemingly endless technical problems, he saw that there was never an idle worker at the site. "Every man on the company payroll," commented a Cimarron observer, "is working with enthusiasm as though the success of the project depends on him."

Yet the completion of the dam dragged on. Severe winter freezes made it impossible to lay cement during a large portion of the year. Moreover, the outbreak of World War I and the subsequent shortages in labor and materials constantly slowed the work. But when the last yard of concrete had finally dried by

View above the completed Eagle Nest Dam looking east
down the Cimarron River valley.

National Scouting Museum Collection, Cimarron, New Mexico.

1920, Charles Springer and all of northern New Mexico could boast of a well-built, effectively designed irrigation system.

With year-round water supplies assured to them for the first time, many ranchers could breathe a sigh of relief. An era of insecurity had ended for pioneers such as H.M. Porter, William French, and Charles Springer's own CS Ranch. At last the arid climate and irregular precipitation of northern New Mexico had been overcome by the ingenuity and perseverance of man.

Railroads into Colfax County

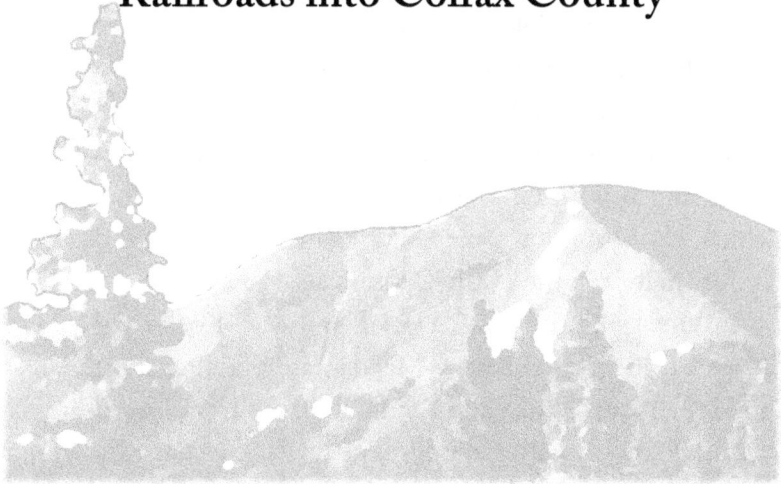

The Coming of the Iron Horse

Despite the prosperity which apparently typified the Colfax County region at the dawn of the twentieth century, inadequate transportation facilities threatened to curtail development. Cattlemen with thousands of fattened stock ready for market now found it difficult to reach the East. Fruit growers were confronted with increasingly large difficulties in transporting their apples, pears, and cherries to consumers. Mining men required modern transportation to ship complex ores to distant smelters and to import heavy mining machinery.

Without economical transportation the area along the edge of the Sangre de Cristos would soon sink into that class of broken, worthless communities which already cluttered the West. Everyone thought that railroads would solve the transportation dilemma and assure continued prosperity. The people of northern New Mexico were determined that such roads would be built.

Numerous railroads had announced plans to penetrate the heart of the county, connecting with the Santa Fe railroad somewhere south of Raton Pass. As early as 1872 the North and South Railroad Company said it planned to connect Cimarron with Kit Carson, Colorado, and El Paso, Texas. Then the Arkansas Valley and Cimarron Railroad hoped to run up the Arkansas River Valley, while the Colorado and Southern connection would run south through Ponil Park into Cimarron. Even more promising was the Cimarron River and Taos Valley Railroad which would run from the Santa Fe mainline to Elizabethtown. Unfortunately, none of these plans came to fruition.

In July 1902 Thomas P. Harlan and Max Koehler of St. Louis arrived in northern New Mexico, announcing their plans to build the New Mexico and Pacific Railroad from Raton to Elizabethtown, eventually extending to the Pacific coast. Incorporated in September of that year, the company soon had surveyors in the field. After many delays a party of prominent St. Louis capitalists arrived for a personal inspection tour of the surveyed route in October 1903. The financiers were met by a brass band at Elizabethtown and warmly welcomed everywhere, but still construction did not commence.

Not until 1905 were the Missouri men back in northern New Mexico, now reorganized as the St. Louis, Rocky Mountain, and Pacific Railroad Company. They had diverted their interests from the gold mines and agricultural lands of the Cimarron district to the coal beds near Raton. They still planned to build to Taos, however, and in September 1905 let grading contracts to the Utah Construction Company which would build over one-hundred miles of track connecting Raton with the Colorado and Southern at Des Moines, New Mexico, and with Cimarron to the west.

Work progressed slowly and it was not until December 10, 1906, that the first train was able to race from Raton into Cimarron. For several days ranchers, miners, Indians, and others had been pouring into the little town to celebrate the arrival of the iron horse. The train whistle was heard in the distance and the flag-draped train pulled into Cimarron with a full load of dignitaries. A new era had dawned.

Soon the Rocky Mountain Line was hauling passengers, freight, and coal to and from the area in its 536 cars, with five freight and two passenger locomotives. All were emblazoned with the red swastika symbol adopted as the road's trademark.

The Swastika Route

In addition to the importance of having a railroad penetrate the heart of Colfax County, Cimarron and its neighbors also benefitted from the location of the railroad's maintenance shops. A roundhouse was under construction by January 1907 and a turntable, pits, and all necessary machinery were soon installed. The shops were under the management of Master Mechanic J.W. Records, and they were equipped to construct and repair all the

St. Louis, Rocky Mountain, and Pacific Railway depot in Cimarron, showing the water tank and an eastbound train departing the station.

Aztec Mill Museum Collection, Cimarron, New Mexico.

127

Rocky Mountain equipment. The machine shop could cut, drill, shear, and punch the heaviest metal available. By mid-1907 Records would exhibit a fifteen-ton derrick built at the plant, and the company could boast of the excellent conditions of locomotives, cars, and equipment.

Despite their elaborate plans, railroad officials soon realized that there was insufficient passenger traffic between Cimarron and Ute Park to justify a regularly scheduled train there. Instead, they ordered a twelve-passenger gasoline driven motor car in May 1907 to service the western end of the line. A month later the vehicle arrived from Chicago and quickly became the talk of Cimarron as it rolled toward Ute Park on its inaugural trip. Canopied and curtained to protect riders from the weather, the little car reached Ute Park in fifty minutes, returning to Cimarron in just over one-half hour.

To stimulate business west of Cimarron the company arranged to open a resort in scenic Ute Park, where local Indians had once camped and miners still prospected. Plans called for the immediate construction of a large pavilion, with glass windows and porches to facilitate the enjoyment of the canyon's beauty throughout the year. A lunch counter would serve meals to visitors and rest rooms "furnished with the utmost comfort and taste" would provide for relaxation.

The resort, famed as one of the most beautiful in the southern Rockies, opened in the early summer of 1908. A special excursion train carried Raton residents to the park, where they witnessed an exciting baseball contest between teams from Cimarron and the coal town of Van Houten. Later the crowd moved inside and danced to the music of a fine band. A sumptuous meal followed. The inaugural crowd was smaller than expected, but everyone seemed certain that the ideal climate and superb scenery of the area would attract additional visitors.

Passengers posing with the Swastika Route caboose.

Aztec Mill Museum Collection, Cimarron, New Mexico.

There were increasing rumors that one of the large railroads was interested in the Rocky Mountain Route, and this was confirmed when the Atchison, Topeka, and Santa Fe company purchased the line. News of the sale was not all good, however, for the Santa Fe immediately decided to service all cars in its Raton shops. The Cimarron roundhouse and machine shops were moved to Raton by early 1914. The railroad continued to operate independently until 1915 when it was merged into the Santa Fe system and its name changed to the Rocky Mountain and Santa Fe.

A ride on the Old Swastika Route was something never to be forgotten. After an exciting and sometimes dangerous trip through the scenic mountains, the big locomotive pulled into the Ute Park station by late afternoon. None of the imposing tourist facilities envisioned by local residents met the eye. Even the spacious summer homes which now grace the area had not yet been built. Only a small railroad depot existed, which was operated by agent F.B. Strong, who also ran a general store while serving as postmaster and game warden for the area.

After completing work for the day, the railroad employees could find a pole and do some fishing. The more ambitious might hike to the top of the canyon and gaze at the natural spectacle of rushing water and rock cliffs. After such exertion, the complete relaxation of a night at Ute Park was most inviting.

Long-time railroad employee Ed Mahoney wrote, "Spending a night in Ute Park was something like camping out, but with all the conveniences. That was really living! No distracting noises, pressures, or interruptions. At that elevation...one sleeps under blankets even in summer. The only night sounds were soothing ones—the wind in the pines and the murmur of the stream." These sentiments, since echoed by thousands of visitors, still make Ute Park a most pleasant place to spend a few days or months.

Producing Ties and Timber

The penetration of Colfax County by the iron horse also made possible the exploitation of the vast timber resources north of Cimarron. Along the sides of many narrow valleys and on the mesas nearby, thousands of acres of timber awaited harvest, consisting mainly of Ponderosa pine and Douglas fir. With hundreds of newly opened coal mines requiring props and new railroads needing ties, the value of this timber supply suddenly increased.

The canyons through which the Ponil River and its branches flowed were particularly inviting to lumbermen. Located only a few miles north of Cimarron, the north, middle, and south forks of the river were thickly blanketed with large timber stands. The arrival of the St. Louis, Rocky Mountain, and Pacific provided the required transportation for wood products.

The person most interested in developing the timber reserves was Theodore A. Schomburg, a young man who had worked his way up through the ranks of the land grant company. He briefly managed the Rocky Mountain Timber Company in southern Colorado, but early in 1907 he quit to start his own lumber and railroad operation in Cimarron. His Continental Tie and Lumber Company and the Cimarron and Northwestern Railway Company were to have a lasting impact on the region.

Local newspapers were soon trumpeting the company's plans to build a railroad from Cimarron north through Ponil Canyon to Ponil Park. Acquiring right-of-way from landowners, they soon began surveying. The route crossed the Ponil River dozens of times and climbed 1,400 feet in elevation with a maximum grade of only two percent. Built according to the most rigid ICC regulations, it would have a capacity limited only by the power of the locomotives to hold back fully-loaded cars.

To facilitate communication, a telephone line paralleling the tracks was rushed to completion so that surveying, engineering,

Cimarron and Northwestern train preparing to load mine props.
Aztec Mill Museum Collection, Cimarron, New Mexico.

and grading crews could talk with each other. All was in readiness by March 1907 when the first grading contractor began work. In Cimarron the station grounds and storage yards were also being readied.

It was clearly understood from the beginning that the Cimarron and Northwestern was designed solely to haul timber for the CT&L mills in Cimarron. A few passengers and small loads of freight were carried, but these were incidental to the purpose of the railroad. An agreement with the lumber company assured profits to make the combined operation legitimate.

For a small lumber-hauling line, the Cimarron and Northwestern purchased used rolling stock from other parts of the country. Costing over $7,000, a Baldwin locomotive was given the number "1." In addition, five boxcars would haul mine props and thirty-nine flat cars would carry stacked lumber or raw logs. One caboose carried employees and any passengers who might ride the line. Total outlay for equipment exceeded $20,000, bringing the final costs to around $250,000.

By June 13, 1907 the company contractors had laid track out of Cimarron. Six months later, on January 6, 1908, the Cimarron and Northwestern Railway opened over twenty-two miles of track from Cimarron to Ponil Park. Now it was ready to begin exploiting the rich timber resources.

Economic Boom Times

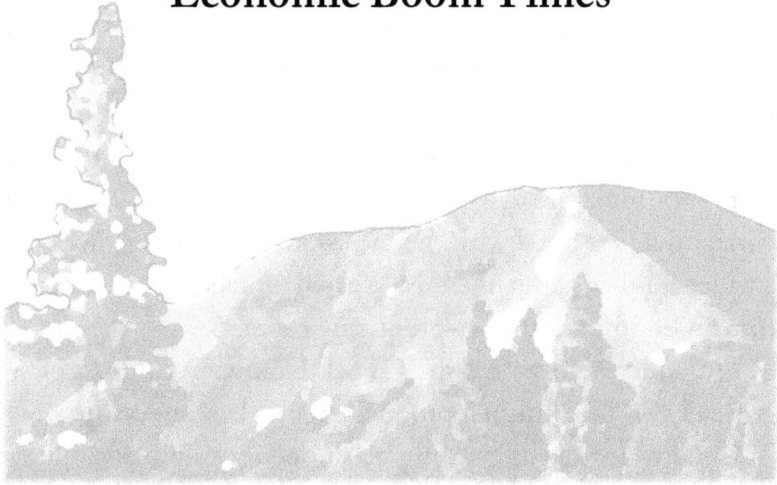

The Lumber Industry is Born

All along the C&N route, the timber foremen established a series of camps. If there was a good-sized stand of trees in the area, a small sawmill might be built. Otherwise, the railroad could haul logs from all along the line to a centrally located mill. After the camp had been selected, a number of men were assigned to work out of it in specified regions. These men usually worked on a commission with pay varying according to the amount of lumber delivered.

Some crews specialized in cutting mine props, leaving the timber naturally round with the bark intact, and using smaller trees or the tops from larger ones for props. Peeled red spruce was the most popular variety for mine entrances because it could withstand the deteriorating effects better than Ponderosa pine. The largest customer for props was the St. Louis, Rocky Mountain, and Pacific Company which needed them for their coal mines.

Some were also used in the gold mines on Baldy Mountain.

A second important product was lumber. Here raw logs were hauled to nearby sawmills using wagons or by skidding them behind stout horses. The sawn timber then went by railroad to Cimarron where a huge planing mill was able to turn out 150,000 board-feet of lumber daily. Special surfaces could be cut, molded, and shaped for every requirement.

A second mill in Cimarron owned by the Cimarron Lumber Company took care of other logs being hauled out of Dean Canyon, and it was fitted with the most modern equipment. Several smaller lumber companies also existed which turned Cimarron into an important lumber-producing center.

The other item which the CT&L Company turned out was railroad ties. The finished products were taken out of the woods to Cimarron where they could be shipped to companies all over the southwest. Much later in 1913, construction was started on a $150,000 tie treating plant which used preservatives, usually zinc chloride, injected under high pressure to permeate the wood

Continental Tie and Lumber Company Planing Mill in Cimarron.

Aztec Mill Museum Collection, Cimarron, New Mexico.

fibers. The plant could treat 1,500 ties daily, and orders for over 100,000 had accumulated within a few months.

As the timber supplies were exhausted along the original C&N route, track was laid into new areas. The first addition came in 1911 when the railroad extended thirteen miles from Ponil Park west and then south to Bonito, where a large new mill was built employing 125 men. Once this area had also been cut, however, the line was slowly abandoned and track was pulled up. By the early 1920s the rails were being reused for a new spur into South Ponil Canyon almost to the base of Baldy Mountain. It enabled the company to cut additional timber from the top of Wilson Mesa and the surrounding areas.

By June 1923 the timber supply in the area served by the C&N was gone. Past experience had shown the managers that extending their rail lines brought only increased expenses and diminished profits. Securing approval from the ICC to close their railroad operations, the company began taking up the rails, although many ties were left in place. The rolling stock was also disposed of and soon the Cimarron and Northwestern was no more.

Schomburg and his associates had made important contributions to Colfax County's economy. Today the locomotive and flatcars are gone from Ponil Canyon, and the sounds of clanging wheels and sharp whistles have vanished, leaving the mountains quiet once again. But the lumber industry continues to be an important economic activity in the area. Trucks have replaced locomotives and flatcars but the industrial potential which these men demonstrated continues to be exploited.

A Boom in Cimarron

The construction of two railroads into the Cimarron area brought great prosperity to the little town in the opening decades of the twentieth century. For the first time in years railroad employees, lumber company workers, and others sought homes in town. To handle such demands, George Remley, Fred Whitney, Charles Springer, and others incorporated the Cimarron Townsite Company, obtaining title to 225 acres north of the Cimarron River. To promote the sale of lots, the group planted hundreds of shade trees along the broad boulevards of "New Town" and donated a whole block to be used as a baseball field.

Soon new buildings were going up all over Cimarron. Duckworth and Marling opened their Oxford Hotel in April 1907, and within two months the level of business necessitated the construction of an addition. H.K. Grubbs announced plans to build a modern theatre with dressing rooms, scenery drops, and the most up-to-date fixtures. When residents complained that the service provided by the Colorado Telephone Company was so poor that is was "almost impossible to carry on an intelligent conversation," a group organized their own company, arranged for long distance connections, and commenced installing phones throughout town. Others decried the poor banking facilities, and soon businessmen had founded the First National Bank of Cimarron and erected a handsome two-story stone and brick building to house it.

Social life also improved. A group of sportsmen joined together to form the Cimarron Athletic Club in the spring of 1909. Twenty-five men pledged to donate fifty dollars to lease a new stone building and remodel it. The first floor would be a gymnasium and training quarters, while the second would house a billiard table, reading room, and assembly hall. Throughout the year the club sponsored numerous sports events, including prize fights, baseball games, and polo exhibitions.

Soon Cimarron boasted a regular baseball team, "The Swastikas," which played in the modern 500-seat ball park wearing their blue jerseys with bright red swastikas across the front. A polo team, which went by the same name, found it difficult to

The Oxford Hotel in Cimarron.

Aztec Mill Museum Collection, Cimarron, New Mexico.

produce either trained ponies or able opponents but played a regular schedule anyway. Not to be outdone, a group of golf enthusiasts laid out links just north of town and announced plans to build a clubhouse and other facilities.

The population increases also encouraged a religious revival, and soon both Protestants and Catholics were undertaking building projects. Catholic citizens, long without a regular meeting place, were urged by Father Sellier of Springer to erect a new place of worship. A Raton architect volunteered to design the building, and members of the parish pledged to make every necessary sacrifice to complete it. In 1909 the Baptists organized, rented a hall in which to hold services, and persuaded Reverend J.A. Cutler to move to Cimarron. The Methodists had more difficulties with their building project. No sooner had they completed construction on a new church than a freak windstorm, said to have been the most severe in three decades, completely destroyed the building. Undaunted by natural calamity, church members determined to rebuild and soon had a new structure ready for occupancy.

Symbolizing the revival were the two weekly newspapers which were published in Cimarron. The *Cimarron News and Press*, which first appeared on January 10, 1907, bore a masthead of the same type used by its namesake in the 1870s. Owned by the Cimarron Publishing Company, it continued to publish for over a decade. On March 4, 1908, the first issue of the *Cimarron Citizen*, edited by George Remley and filled with his townsite advertisements, appeared on the streets. It was apparently less long-lived than its competitor.

The most significant addition to the town during its years of prosperity was a new water system. The work got underway in September 1907 when George H. Webster, Jr., the manager of the Urraca Ranch just south of town, received permission to appropriate the necessary water from Cimarroncito Creek. Three years passed before Webster organized the Cimarron Water Company, designed the reservoir and pipeline system, and began construction. By the spring of 1911 the city could claim one of the finest water facilities in New Mexico.

The Rebirth of Mining

While trains hauled lumber out of Cimarron and a new era of irrigation aided agriculturalists, sounds of activity once more echoed through the canyons around Baldy Mountain. Clangs and creaks again could be heard in tunnels where miners hacked chunks of ore from the mountain's mass and rolled them toward daylight in ponderous carts. Iron stamps crashed down on the gold-rich rock with monotonous regularity. Chattering youngsters, gossiping women, and yapping dogs joined in the chorus that announced the revival of the Colfax County mining district in 1893.

Of the Baldy mines, the largest and most productive had been the Aztec. After a series of unsuccessful efforts to get the mine going during the 1890s, the property finally began to show profits when the Maxwell Land Grant Company employed J.T. Sparks to superintend it in 1909. Sparks was neither a professional engineer nor a practical miner, but he was rough and tough enough to control the men working under him. To give Sparks technical advice, the company officials hired as a consultant a well-known Colorado mining engineer, Charles A. Chase.

It was probably on the recommendation of Chase that Sparks sank four shafts, identified numerically, at intervals of 75 feet along Aztec Ridge. Shaft No. 4 struck a contact formation late in 1911. Several years of work failed to return appreciable profit, however, and when he began to drink excessively, Sparks was replaced by Ernest V. Dehayes, an easterner turned mining engineer who had worked as assayer and surveyor under Sparks.

With Dehayes in charge, the company began a last ditch effort to find the rich ore they suspected must be somewhere along the contact formation. Good news soon arrived. One afternoon

Baldy Town as it appeared in the 1930s.
National Scouting Museum Collection, Cimarron, New Mexico.

139

when the superintendent sent a few samples of shale from No. 4 to the assayer, he was amazed to learn that it was worth nearly $3,000 per ton.

The lode proved so rich that the company's profits surged upward. The manager set another crew to work milling the ore, installing new equipment, and employing additional men. Immediately the Aztec shifted to the credit side of the Dutch corporation's ledgers. The total Colfax County gold production jumped from only $15,588 in 1913 to $350,745 in 1915. Between November 1914 and July the following year, 21,000 tons of ore returned an average of $107.60 per ton to the company's coffers.

Rapid development in the mine and mill generated feverish activity at the little village perched high on the eastern slopes of Baldy Mountain. So many families arrived at Baldy Town that the company was unable to accommodate them and many were compelled to live in tents. Because everyone aspired to work in the mines, men to do necessary construction work were scarce. In July 1916 the Dutchmen contracted with two local builders, Scott and Blakely, to erect a boarding house. Designed to accommodate single men, it would relieve the desperate housing shortage. When the so-called hotel was completed, several hundred guests trekked to Baldy from all over the district to attend a gala housewarming and dance.

While the Aztec was booming, several other mines in the area also saw new activity. On the northern side of the ridge the Claude Mining and Milling Company installed a new mill, bucket tramway, and inside equipment before reopening the French Henry Mine. The Mystic, the Rebel Chief, the Senate-Bobtail, and numerous others opened for short periods.

One of the most curious mining operations was the Black Horse, operated by a colorful Dutchman, "Baron" Philip H. Van Zuylen. Sometimes as owner, other times as superintendent or

Baron Van Zuylen's Black Horse Mine.
National Scouting Museum Collection, Cimarron, New Mexico.

even as a day laborer, Van Zuylen kept at work for almost twenty years. He never married, but saved his money for a trip back to Holland, which he made in 1897. On his return to the district, the baron started back to work in the mine, but when the property became involved in litigation after the turn of the century he moved to Cimarron. In 1908 he was once again planning to resume operations when he received word that he had inherited a large fortune. Although the size of the inheritance was evidently greatly exaggerated, he never returned to active mining operations.

Into the Heart of Baldy

Of all the mining stories, the most exciting and in many ways the saddest concerns the attempts to dig a tunnel all the way through Baldy Mountain. Many local experts had argued for years that somewhere in the heart of the mountain there must be a central source of gold, some "mother lode" which, if it could be located, would prove extremely rich. The first group to consider a tunnel all the way through was organized on February 27, 1899, as the E-Town Tunnel Company, but its plans were never put into action. In the fall of 1900 two brothers, Alexander and William McIntyre, joined Leroy Burt to incorporate a company of their own, the Gold and Copper Deep Tunnel Mining and Milling Company.

The McIntyres' plans were as formidable as their company name. They would start at the top of Big Nigger Gulch above Elizabethtown and bore 3,000 feet into the mountain in a north-westerly direction, reaching a depth of 1,800 feet. Within a few weeks several "commodious" buildings had been erected and two shifts put to work at the task. The drilling and blasting proceeded slowly and after seven years they had completed only 2,000 feet of the work.

For many years during the early twentieth century, the two brothers continued their efforts. Forced to stop work in 1908 for lack of funds, they pushed on two years later. By 1912 they had

Employee Jim Glassen (left) and William McIntyre (right) standing at the western entrance of the Deep Tunnel Mine on Baldy Mountain.

National Scouting Museum Collection, Cimarron, New Mexico.

issued and sold another $200,000 worth of stock and promptly spent all the money. Within the next fourteen years an additional $90,000 was raised and spent.

When Bill Brewster, a nephew of the McIntyres who resided in Cimarron as this was being written, went to the mine in 1921, he saw the results of many of those expenditures. A small mining community had been established at the head of the gulch. The superintendent's house, two-story bunk house for the workers, cook shack, dining hall, power building, blacksmith shop, and a large edifice containing a 100-ton mill marked the entrance to the Deep Tunnel.

In the decade that followed, the two brothers sold just enough additional stock to pay for driving their tunnel further into the heart of the mountain. They were constantly optimistic, always certain that they would soon encounter those elusive veins. The men never struck it rich. After William McIntyre died of pneumonia in a Raton hospital in 1930, his brother continued the project alone.

Two years later, employees of the Deep Tunnel Mining and Milling Company appeared at the headwaters of South Ponil Creek to start work on a second tunnel, designed to join the first tunnel deep inside Baldy. A young geologist, Alvis F. Denison, began by running a transit line over the mountain from one side to the other, establishing an exact starting point for the new entrance. Following Denison's instructions, work on the tunnel was soon underway.

On February 8, 1936, the two tunnels met with such remarkable precision that only an inch separated their centers. But with the trans-mountain underpass complete, all hopes of finding the mother lode were abandoned. When a visitor climbed up to the once active mine headquarters in 1940, he found a "deserted village where men had lived and hoped and worked." The old ore cars, warped and rusty from disuse, still rested on tracks running into the mine. Although it was possible even then for a visitor to walk straight through Baldy Mountain, he would see no rich veins along the way. The Deep Tunnel Mining and Milling Company had been a colossal failure, exhausting the money of many investors and the lives of William and Alex McIntyre.

The tragic history of the Deep Tunnel continued more recently. During the spring and summer of 1965-66 an El Paso, Texas, company began to reexamine the mine. This time they looked not for gold but for uranium and molybdenum. The venture ended suddenly when they broke through a dike which let a flood of accumulated water rush toward the entrance. One man lost his life in the tragedy, and a second received serious injuries. With the State Mine Inspector claiming that they had violated safety requirements, the new exploiters abandoned their efforts in the Deep Tunnel and left the area.

Gentlemen Ranchers and Tourists

The End of Gold Mining in Colfax County

Mining continued to be an important economic activity in Colfax County until the outbreak of World War II. Few rich veins or placer grounds were discovered, but hundreds of miners continued to work in small, low-profit operations which supported them and their families.

The largest and most productive mine was the Aztec, operated under the direct management of the Maxwell Land Grant Company. It installed new machinery and began to use more scientific techniques during the 1920s. Reopening in the late 1930s, it continued to produce quantities of gold ore until 1940. A thriving community near the mill site housed a hundred or more residents for many years.

Yet the Aztec seemed to be operating on borrowed time. Occasionally a rich ore pocket was discovered, but they were seldom very extensive. Much effort was devoted to finding new ore, but these met with only limited success. Moreover, the Dutch company became increasingly reluctant to pour money into the enterprise. Replacing manager Matt Gorman with a Dutchman, Victor J. Van Lint, the corporation was determined that the mine must either pay its own way or be closed. Friction between Van Lint and his employees made it even more difficult to establish a profitable operation. Finally, federal regulations regarding the price of gold and the wages which must be paid to miners further reduced profits.

By the summer of 1940 Van Lint was at last ready to admit that the Aztec had become a liability. Holland had been overrun by German armies and certainly the Dutch stockholders could no longer operate a mine in America which did not even pay expenses. Consequently the mine and mill ceased operation on September 1, 1940. Two weeks later the little town was virtually abandoned. By early 1941 its houses had been demolished, the mill machinery sold, and rails, pipe, and everything else of value hauled away. Baldy Town was no more.

The entrance of America into World War II marked the end of all significant mining work in the Baldy district. Since 1942 a few lone prospectors have sluiced small quantities of precious metal from the Moreno Valley, but never since then has the amount exceeded $500 per year. Across the great mountain at the headwaters of Ute Creek, a scene of desertion greeted the visitor to Baldy Town. Only the crumbling walls of the old store and the majestic mountain itself broke the monotony of over-grown mine dumps and shafts.

Across the mountain, Elizabethtown suffered a similar fate. Several placer mining operations using new mechanized meth-ods had been operating in the Moreno Valley during the 1930s, but with the outbreak of war, these were forced to close down. The Fullroe Company of Ohio abandoned its efforts in 1942. Soon afterward the Peerless Mining Company also closed down.

Ruins of the Mutz Hotel in Elizabethtown,
as it appeared in the early 1940s.
Library of Congress Prints and Photographs Division, Public Domain Images.

The people who once lived in Elizabethtown have moved to Eagle Nest, where fishermen, winter sports enthusiasts, and sightseers support a year-round population. Visiting the abandoned village in 1953 one writer described Elizabethtown's buildings filled with memories of the past:

> E-Town may come alive in the summer, when fishermen and tourists roam the mountains and cattlemen drive their herds into the fertile valley and up the slopes of Old Baldy, but in February it is only a rattling husk.

Gentleman Ranchers

Visitors have gloried in the natural beauty of Colfax County since the earliest days of the Santa Fe Trail. Cold mountain streams offered fishing unexcelled in the Rocky Mountain West, and cool breezes brought welcome relief from the hot summers which predominate in much of America. Majestic mountains and dramatic rock formations awed everyone who saw them.

During the first decades of the twentieth century a band of wealthy men began to take advantage of the scenic wonders of northern New Mexico. Having made large fortunes elsewhere, these men bought huge ranches, built magnificent homes, and spent all or part of the year in the area. Stanley McCormick, under whose direction many irrigation projects had been started, was one of the first of the wealthy ranchers. To the north, William H. Bartlett, a Chicago grain broker, developed the Vermejo Ranch into one of the most exclusive retreats in the West. Three magnificent residences, a glass-covered greenhouse, swimming pools, miles of fine trails, and a beautiful indoor tennis court were included. Such luxury eventually attracted numerous famous people to Colfax County. Included among them were Cecil B. DeMille, Douglas Fairbanks, Harvey G. Firestone, Andrew Mellon, and others.

Almost as luxurious was the ranch complex built by Waite Phillips, an Oklahoma oilman who became interested in Colfax Country during the 1920s. His initial purchase of the George H. Webster ranch was soon followed by the acquisition of many other tracts. At one time Phillips owned almost 300,000 acres. For a summer home, he built a magnificent Mediterranean-style home, the Villa Philmonte, decorated by European artisans and including every modern luxury. Phillips also entertained many famous people, including US Vice President Charles Dawes, who spent several weeks on the property. The famous writers Ben Ames Williams and Kenneth L. Roberts described their vacations at the Phillips ranch in articles for the *Saturday Evening Post*.

Waite Phillips holding his son Elliot (center), with
Wiley Post (left) and Will Rogers (right), late 1920s.
National Scouting Museum Collection, Cimarron, New Mexico.

Numerous activities in the area catered to the interests of
Phillips, the Vermejo Ranch visitors, and other wealthy tourists
in the Sangre de Cristos. A polo club in Cimarron was renowned
as one of the best in the region, with stables and practice grounds
which became major attractions for several area ranches. Under
the leadership of John J. Nairn, an eastern rugmaker's son who
settled close to Phillips, the Maverick Club became the area's
most exclusive social group. Its monthly meetings, frequently
attended by famous visitors to the area, and its annual rodeo
became major activities in northern New Mexico.

A Paradise for Tourists

The wonders of Colfax County were never reserved exclusively for the wealthy. While men like Phillips, Bartlett, and Nairn were hosting private parties on their ranches, thousands of other people were taking advantage of the scenic beauty and natural wonders of northern New Mexico.

Phillips made possible much of this through his philanthropic efforts. Concerned that more people should enjoy the area where his ranch was located, he made an initial gift of 35,000 acres and $61,000 to the Boy Scouts of America in 1937. The Philturn Rockymountain Scoutcamp which the BSA created was so popular that Phillips increased the gift to 127,000 acres in 1941. To keep the cost of attending as low as possible, he also provided as an endowment the Philtower office building in downtown Tulsa, Oklahoma. In 1964 the ranch grew by 10,000 acres with the purchase of a large portion of the old Baldy Mountain mining region, including the Aztec Mine and the site of Baldy Town.

Because of Phillips' generosity, thousands of Scouts, their parents, and leaders flock to Colfax County each year from all over

A group of backpackers enjoying the high country.
Steve Lewis Collection.

the United States and many foreign countries. A visit to Philmont usually means a ten-day backpacking trip, hiking, camping, fishing, and partaking in many programs portraying the area's history and teaching practical outdoor activities. Adults come to the ranch for specialized training in youth leadership. The former Phillips mansion is now one of several museums dedicated to the history of the area.

Cimarron Canyon and Eagle Nest Lake provide other attractions for visitors to Colfax County. Part of the magnificent canyon, highlighted by the Palisades, has been developed as a New Mexico State Park and equipped with many beautiful campsites. A day fishing along the Cimarron River, climbing the canyon walls, or just marvelling at the scenery cannot be excelled anywhere. Eagle Nest Lake is a fishing and boating center in northeastern New Mexico. For a small fee the tourist can spend a few hours or an entire vacation seeking mountain trout in the beautiful surroundings.

Skiing is the most recent of Colfax County's attractions. For years the Red River Resort has offered winter sports to thousands of enthusiasts. The opening of Angel Fire Ski Basin in the southeastern corner of the Moreno Valley extended these activities.

For those interested in exploring the historic past of Colfax County there is also much to do. The Santa Fe Trail Museum in Springer brings together an intriguing assortment of relics from the past. The Raton Museum emphasizes the historical development of the northern part of the county. Everywhere there are old buildings, mines, and other relics that await discovery. Although visitors must be cautious and avoid trespassing, the opportunities for individual exploration are almost unlimited.

About This Edition

For several decades this book has been a popular history describing the important people, places, and events in the northeastern corner of New Mexico. The author, Lawrence R. Murphy, was a meticulous researcher and writer who eventually authored dozens of books and articles on the history of the American West. But some of his most endearing and enduring work is contained in this short compilation of historical sketches, as explained below in the publisher's original forward to the first edition.

Forward to the Original 1969 Edition

Larry Murphy, the author of *Out in God's Country*, has endeavored to show the progress, the heartbreaks, and the dreams of many a pioneer vanished. Originally the contents of this book were published in *The Springer Tribune* in a series entitled "Colfax County Sketches." Larry Murphy has taken us through the history of Colfax County from the beginning of the Ponil people to its present. Truly, the residents of early Colfax County lived here in God's Country, as we do today.

The author received his PhD in history from Texas Christian University and at present is assistant professor of history at Western Illinois University at Macomb, Illinois, where he teaches American history and history of the West. Larry Murphy has worked for many years at the Philmont Scout Ranch, which sparked his passion for the history of the region.

We have dedicated the book to the memory of Narciso Abreu whose acquaintance and conversations I will treasure always. The poem "The Book of Life" that is printed here was brought to me by Mr. Abreu scribbled on a piece of paper, and it is signed *Anonymous*. I believe that Mr. Abreu was therein writing his own eulogy, because shortly afterward he passed away.

It has been our privilege and pleasure to publish this book. It is the most current and readable history of Colfax County, New Mexico. I hope you enjoy your trek through history "Out in God's Country."

Carlos Gutierrez, Publisher
Springer Tribune

Dedicated to the Memory of
Narciso McCoy Abreu
1877 - 1968
Pioneer, Gentleman, Friend

The Book of Life

It's a good thing the Book of Life
Can be turned one page at a time.
Some claim it is all written for us long before our births.
Others hold that we will write it all ourselves,
That we all unconsciously form the plot and
Make of it a tragedy or a farce.
As for myself—I would not snip a page,
Nor would I wish to turn today to the chapter ahead
To see if there might be for me sunshine tomorrow.
Anonymous

Recollections of the Gutierrez Family

As we write this dedication to Carlos and Valentina Gutierrez, we are reminded of the many gifts that they received and that they bestowed upon so many. If we could sum it up in a single word, that word is *opportunity*.

Dad was given the opportunity by Mr. Ed Guthman to work at the *Springer Tribune* press when he was just eleven years old. It led to a lifelong love of printing and eventual ownership of the *Tribune*. Dad took the opportunity to mentor those interested in the printing trade, including some students from the New Mexico Boy's School.

Mom and Dad had the opportunity to meet at our Uncle Con and Aunt Lucille's wedding. Even though they didn't correspond for several years after that, they met again and married in 1956, and their life together and their partnership lasted nearly 56 years. Mom and Dad raised five daughters, providing the opportunity for all of us to become college graduates with strong careers, while providing an excellent example of family love.

There was a young historian, Larry Murphy, who asked for the opportunity to write a historical account of Colfax County, and Mom and Dad took that opportunity to publish it in the *Springer Tribune* as the weekly series, "Colfax County Sketches." Our aunt suggested they publish the sketches in book form for all to enjoy, so Mom and Dad followed that advice and published *Out in God's Country* for the first time in 1969.

Carlos and Valentina Gutierrez were a remarkable team who had opportunities and gave opportunities to so many. We have been blessed to call them Dad and Mom.

August 1, 2021   Mary Grace Gutierrez Smigiel
Marie Adele Gutierrez Baca   Lorraine Gutierrez
Dolores Gutierrez DeHerrera   Nancy Gutierrez Suazo

Recollections of the Davis Family

We would like to thank the Gutierrez sisters for entrusting us with the next generation of *Out In God's Country*. Following Carlos' death, the girls had a family counsel and decided they wanted the publication of the history of Colfax County to continue. They felt we fellow-natives of the area would be good custodians of their parents' legacy.

We have fond memories of many trips with our Dad, Les Davis, to *The Springer Tribune* to see Carlos and pick up a batch of freshly-printed books. Dad gave copies of the book to all visitors on the CS Ranch and featured them at the Aztec Mill Museum in Cimarron. Mom and Dad were lifelong friends and political allies of Carlos and Valentina.

Decades later, we bought the historic Rosso Mercantile in Old Town Cimarron. Renovations were completed in the summer of 2020 and we opened the Cimarron Mercantile and Café. We envision the Mercantile as a community hub where people can gather and learn together, one that preserves and promotes the history and heritage of this beautiful region of New Mexico that we call God's Country.

October, 2021   Linda M. Davis
Julia D. Stafford   Kimberly K. Barmann

A Tribute to Lawrence R. Murphy

Larry Murphy first arrived in Colfax County, New Mexico, in June 1961 to work on the summer staff at Philmont Scout Ranch. He had just graduated from high school in Sacramento, California, where he excelled in academics. Although he suffered from severe asthma, the climate of the high country agreed with him. Like many before him, he became passionate about the history of the American West while working in a place that inspires the imagination with visions of life during pioneer times. For a decade Larry would return to the region summer after summer, serving on the program staff at Philmont while pursuing academic degrees during the school year. He was awarded a B.A. in History from the University of Arizona in 1964, and in 1965 Larry earned an M.A. in History after completing his thesis entitled *Boom and Bust on Baldy Mountain, New Mexico, 1864-1942*. He enrolled in the doctoral program at Texas Christian University in the autumn of 1965 and emerged in 1968 with a Ph.D. in History.

In 1969 Larry accepted his first academic teaching position at Western Illinois University as Assistant Professor of American History and History of the West. In 1972 the University of New Mexico Press published his landmark book, *Philmont: A History of New Mexico's Cimarron Country*, which is still in print today.

Larry advanced to Associate Professor in 1973 and to full Professor in 1979, after which he was recruited to serve as Dean of Continuing Education at the University of the Pacific. There Larry Murphy himself became a pioneer in the new field of Continuing Education, a program for meeting the needs of non-traditional students desiring to take university courses to enhance their personal knowledge and skills.

Narciso Abreu visiting with Larry Murphy in the late 1960s.

In 1981 he moved to Central Michigan University, where he served as Director of the Institute for Personal and Career Development, and in 1985 Larry became Dean of the College of Lifelong Learning at Wayne State University in Detroit. On September 26, 1987, shortly before his forty-fifth birthday, he was attending a banquet in honor of donors to the school and was about to take the podium when he collapsed and died from an acute pulmonary attack.

Larry Murphy's life was cut short, but his personal impact and his legacy in writing continue to touch lives to this day. Like his long-time friend and fellow historian David L. Caffey, Larry had a special gift for making complex historical details clear and understandable for readers of all backgrounds. While being precise and historically accurate, his writing style is always engaging and thoroughly enjoyable. It is our hope that this updated edition of *Out in God's Country* will give Larry Murphy's legacy a new surge of life for today's readers.

Suggested Reading

Armstrong, Ruth. *The Chases of Cimarron*. New Mexico Stockman, 1981.

Caffey, David L. *Frank Springer and New Mexico*. Texas A&M University Press, 2006.

Cleaveland, Agnes Morley. *Satan's Paradise*. Houghton Mifflin, 1952.

Fergusson, Harvey. *Grant of Kingdom: a Novel*. University of New Mexico Press, 1975.

Freiberger, Harriet. *Lucien Maxwell: Villain or Visionary*. Eagle Trail Press, 2016.

Keleher, William A. *Maxwell Land Grant: A New Mexico Item*. University of New Mexico Press, 1983, or Sunstone Press reprint, 2008.

MacDonald, Randall M., Lamm, Gene, and MacDonald, Sarah E. *Cimarron and Philmont*. Arcadia Publishing, 2012.

Murphy, Lawrence R. *Lucien Bonaparte Maxwell: Napoleon of the Southwest*. University of Oklahoma Press, 1983.

—— *Philmont: A History of New Mexico's Cimarron Country*. University of New Mexico Press, 1972 & 2014.

Pearson, Jim Berry. *The Maxwell Land Grant*. University of Oklahoma Press, 1961.

Stanley, F. *The Grant That Maxwell Bought*. World Press, 1952, or Sunstone Press reprint, 2008.

Zimmer, Stephen. *People of the Cimarron Country*. Eagle Trail Press, 2012.

Zimmer, Stephen and Lamm, Gene. *Colfax County*. Arcadia Publishing, 2015.

Zimmer, Stephen and Lewis, Steve. *It Happened in the Cimarron Country*. Eagle Trail Press, 2013.

Zimmer, Stephen and Walker, Larry. *Philmont: An Illustrated History*. Boy Scouts of America, 1988.

www.ingramcontent.com/pod-product-compliance
Lightning Source LLC
LaVergne TN
LVHW051347080426
835509LV00020BA/3330